BRITISH RAILWAYS

PAST and PRESENT

No 20

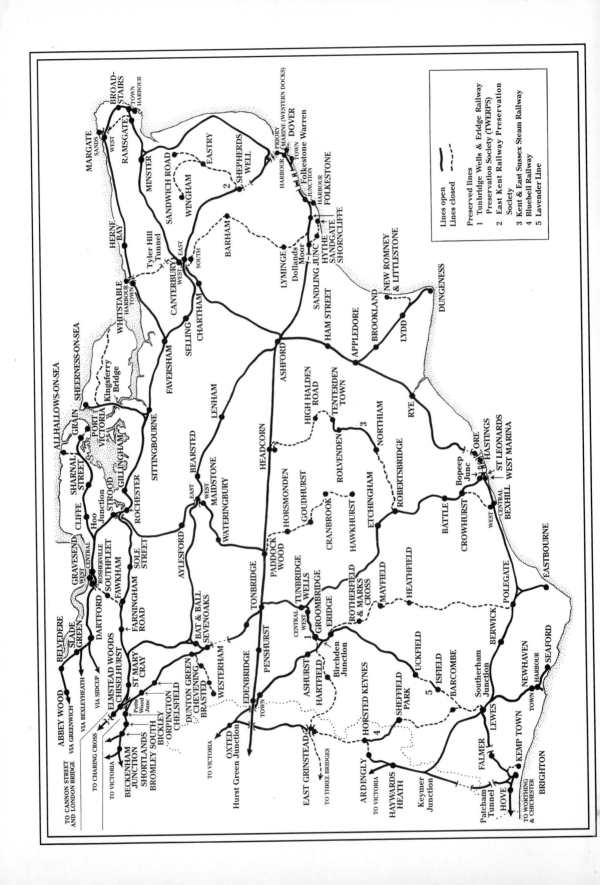

BRITISH RAILWAYS

PAST and PRESENT

No 20

Kent and East Sussex

Brian Morrison & Brian Beer

Past and
Present

Past & Present Publishing Ltd

First published in May 1994

British Library Cataloguing in Publication Data

A catalogue record for this book is available from the British Library

ISBN 1 85895 044 9

Past & Present Publishing Ltd
Unit 5
Home Farm Close
Church Street
Wadenhoe
Peterborough PE8 5TE
Tel/fax (0832) 720440

Photographs credited 'BB' were taken by Brian Beer, those credited 'BM' by Brian Morrison.

Maps drawn by Christina Siviter

Printed and bound in Great Britain

SOLE STREET: The station at Sole Street opened shortly after the London, Chatham & Dover Railway (LC&DR) extended the East Kent line towards the capital in 1860. It is situated close to the highest point on the LC&DR main line, and gave its name to the 5-mile climb of 1 in 100 from Rochester Bridge to the east. Starting the ascent on 14 May 1959, Maunsell three-cylinder Class 'N1' 'Mogul' No 31880 powers an express from Ramsgate.

At exactly the same position on a dull 11 July 1992, one of InterCity Sector's fleet of long-range fuel tank Class '47/4s', No 47811, heads the 14.12 Dover Western Docks to Liverpool Lime Street 'InterCity Holidaymaker Express'. The bank on the left has been taken over by foliage, and the wooded area on the right has been replaced by a number of ugly-looking industrial complexes. The chimney centre stage has gone, but at the top right-hand corner of the scene, the parapets of Rochester Castle are still evident. *Dr P. Ransome-Wallis/BB*

CONTENTS

BIBLIOGRAPHY

The Railways of South East England *by Andrew Knight (Ian Allan)*

A Regional History of the Railways of Great Britain, Volume 2, Southern England *by H. P. White (David St John Thomas)*

Jowett's Railway Atlas *by Alan Jowett (Patrick Stephens Limited)*

PSL Field Guide: Railways of the Southern Region *by Geoffrey Body (Patrick Stephens Limited)*

Encyclopaedia of British Railway Companies *by Christopher Awdry (Patrick Stephens Limited)*

Southern Sheds in Camera *by Roger Griffiths (Oxford Publishing Co)*

BR Steam Motive Power Depots, SR *by Paul Bolger (Ian Allan)*

British Railways Workshops *by Edgar Larkin (Oxford Publishing Co)*

Clinker's Register of Closed Passenger Stations *by C. R. Clinker (Avon Anglia)*

British Railways Past and Present: London *by Brian Morrison & Ken Brunt (Past & Present Publishing Ltd)*

Southern Electric Multiple Units by Colin J. Marsden (Ian Allan)

Railway Magazine, Railway World *and* Trains Illustrated *magazines*

SEAFORD: Following powers obtained by the Brighton, Lewes & Hastings Railway in 1846, a branch from Southerham Junction, near Lewes, was opened to Newhaven in December of the following year and extended to Seaford, 2½ miles away, in 1864. At the Seaford terminus on 7 October 1962 London, Brighton & South Coast Railway (LB&SCR) Billinton-designed Class 'E4' 0-6-2T No 32479 heads an enthusiast's special at the island platform, with a Southern Railway 2HAL electric multiple unit (EMU) in the adjacent siding.

Currently the small seaside resort enjoys a half-hourly service from Brighton, usually consisting of Class '421' 4CIG units. On 18 September 1993 No 1705 departs, forming the 15.04 train for Brighton. Very little appears to have changed over the intervening years. *Terry Gough/BM*

INTRODUCTION

Where once 'Schools', 'Battle of Britain', Maunsell 'Mogul' and Wainwright 'C' Class 0-6-0 locomotives proliferated, along with a variety of bone-shaking electric multiple units of varying vintage, the railways of Kent and the eastern parts of Sussex are now thought by many to consist solely of electric trains from London to the coastal towns, and of similarly operated suburban services. Certainly these trains are of considerable importance, but the lines within this south-eastern part of the United Kingdom remain quite complex, and include cross-country services, a considerable amount of freight, some remaining branch lines - and the Channel Tunnel trains yet to come, although a few precursors in this respect are included within these pages.

Present-day views of photographs taken years before vary considerably. Apart from the motive power, some locations have seen very little change, whereas others are unrecognisable. Generally speaking the main lines remain, but a number of the branches have gone, and others are now in the welcome hands of preservationists. It is no longer possible to travel by rail to Gravesend West, Westerham, Tunbridge Wells West, Hawkhurst, All Hallows, Lydd, Hythe, Bexhill West, Kemp Town, or on the Cuckoo Line, but the Kent & East Sussex Railway remains within the bounds of this volume, as does the southern portion of the Bluebell Line at Sheffield Park, the East Kent Railway, and the Lavender Line, truncated at Uckfield, but still in existence around Isfield.

Nearly all of the various 'Southern' engine sheds have disappeared, although remains of some can still be seen. Just two, Slade Green and Ramsgate, survive to attend to the needs of modern traction, and these are now known as traction depots. Tunbridge Wells West still survives to serve the future needs of the Tunbridge Wells & Eridge Railway Preservation Society, and the old repair shops building at St Leonards also houses preserved motive power of more modern variety. The two works complexes within the boundaries of this book are Ashford and Brighton; most of the Ashford buildings remain in use in one way or another, but the Brighton site is now a large car park.

British Rail officials of many grades have been extremely helpful in providing opportunities to photograph many of the present-day scenes from within BR fences, and similarly members of the public have also been extremely courteous in allowing us on to properties that are now their private domain. Just how future owners of track, rolling-stock or services under privatisation will react to such requests for access, however, remains to be seen.

In most cases throughout this volume, the modern view is fairly exact, with feet planted firmly in the same position as dictated by the photographer from years past. In a few locations, however, elevation has gone, and in a few other instances the foliage has forced a slightly different angle to be taken, or in some instances has resulted in the quest having to be aborted altogether.

Unlike the London volumes of 'British Railways Past and Present', where the majority of the views from the past were from my own cameras or from those of Dick Riley, this time the assistance of a number of friends and acquaintances has been needed for the past material, and in this respect grateful thanks go to the many names that appear under their respective pictures throughout the book, or to the custodians of the picture collections. Customary but grateful thanks are also due to Derek Mercer, who has yet again managed to produce many silk purse prints from a number of sow's ear negatives.

Brian Morrison, Sidcup   **Brian Beer, London**

LYMINGE: Incorporated in 1881, the Elham Valley Light Railway was authorised to build a line from Canterbury to Shorncliffe. The company, however, was taken over by the South Eastern Railway (SER) in 1884, and the Elham Valley line eventually opened as far as Barham in 1887, and throughout in 1889. Passenger traffic was never heavy, but after bus competition was introduced on the road that paralleled the route, only a reasonable volume of agricultural traffic kept the line open. This also diminished, however, and final closure came about in October 1947. Photographs of the line have not proved easy to come by, and this rather poor view of a Wainwright Class 'H' 0-4-4T in Lyminge station was copied from an old postcard. Minus platform canopy and chimneys, the station building still remains today, utilised by Lyminge Library. *Lens of Sutton/BM*

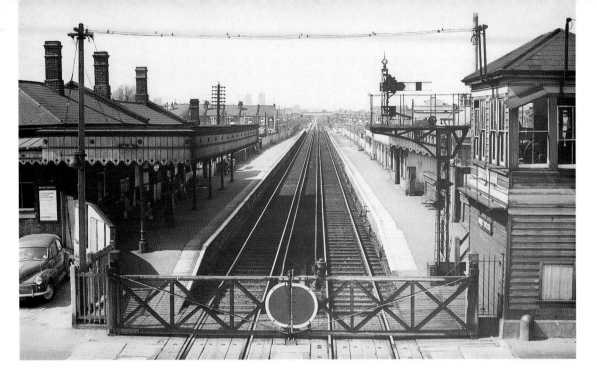

North Kent Line

ABBEY WOOD: As well as being the first station to be listed in the BR Passenger Timetable index, Abbey Wood also marks the boundary between the London and Kent postal districts. In fact, the trains depicted on this page are strictly in London - but the photographers are in Kent! Contrasting with the scene of April 1969, when Abbey Wood boasted a signal box, level crossing and semaphore signals, the June 1993 view shows the newly rebuilt station with a Class '415/6' 4EPB EMU No 5612 in the platform, forming the 10.47 North Kent Line service from Cannon Street to Dartford via Greenwich. The line of houses in the middle distance survives, and the two far tower blocks have increased to eight. *Lawrie Bowles/BB*

BELVEDERE: Platform extensions to accommodate 12-coach 'Networker' EMUs provide the main difference between these two photographs, taken on a murky day in 1970 and on a much brighter-looking day in 1993, although the signal box has gone, the telegraph poles are no more and a number of high-rise flats now show on the skyline. The building and chimney on the left remain, however, together with the houses on the right, where the gasholder also survives. The old 2BIL EMU No 2115 dates from 1937, and had already been withdrawn when this photograph was taken; it was heading a line of other withdrawn EMUs travelling from Wimbledon Park depot to Slade Green for stripping of component parts - a kamikaze mission!

The Class '47/0', No 47249, is hauling a ballast train from an engineer's possession at London Bridge, and is returning to Hoo Junction. *Both BB*

SLADE GREEN: Although the present North Kent Line was opened by the SER in 1849, the station at Slade Green (or Slades Green as it was known until 1953) was not constructed until July 1900. Looking towards Dartford, the level crossing and attendant gatekeeper's house have both gone since the view of December 1965 was taken, together with the signal box and semaphore signalling. Both ends of a footbridge across the tracks can now be seen at the end of the platforms, and the houses on the right still stand, albeit with the walls now painted white. The stabling point for EMUs in the distance and the overbridge remain unchanged in June 1993. *John Faulkner/BB*

SLADE GREEN SHED: After the amalgamation of the SER and LC&DR to form the South Eastern & Chatham Railway (SE&CR) in 1899, the company constructed an eight-road brick-built engine shed at Slades Green in 1901. When electric units replaced steam passenger workings on the south-eastern suburban lines in 1926, the premises were converted for maintenance of the new trains, and another separate building was erected for heavy repairs, now converted for the maintenance of 'Networker' stock. On 24 April 1926, just prior to steam being ousted from the depot, three 'O' Class 0-6-0s, Nos 333, 392 and 394, stand outside the building together with 'Q1' Class 0-4-4T No 359.

On 30 November 1993 the realigned trackwork outside the re-roofed building is clear of stock, but Class '930' 'Sandite' unit No 930033 looks out into the daylight, and deep inside the depot can just be discerned a Class '465' 'Networker'. The striped shutter doors make it less likely for train drivers entering the building to forget that the doors are there! *H. C. Casserley/BM*

DARTFORD JUNCTION: With three routes from London, via the North Kent Line and the Bexleyheath and Sidcup lines, all converging at Dartford, the junction to the west of the station is a very busy one, with trains often passing every few minutes. On 2 October 1968 the experimental Class 4DD 'double decker' EMUs No 4001/4002 (1949-1971) pass through and approach Dartford station.

On 13 June 1993 an eight-car 'Networker', consisting of units Nos 465205 and 465019, passes the same spot. Semaphore signalling has been replaced by colour lights, two of the three gasholders have gone, and foliage is beginning to obstruct the view. Surprisingly, in these days of British Rail 'rationalisation', the trackwork has actually increased. *John Cooper-Smith/BB*

DARTFORD: The site of Dartford station dates from the opening of the North Kent Line in 1849. The original Italianate design by the architect of London Bridge, Samuel Beazley, has, however, given way to a building of modern design, which is functional but has quite failed to eliminate the effects of a seemingly eternal cold wind that howls around the platform areas in summer and winter alike. On 23 May 1959, prior to rebuilding, the station was host to Wainwright Class 'D1' 4-4-0 No 31743 and a green-liveried 4EPB EMU.

When the scene on 23 October 1993 was recorded, nothing at all remained of the original buildings or their surrounds, other than the platforms themselves. The 4EPB No 5462 is now in Network SouthEast (NSE) livery and classified '415/4', and the Class '465/0' 'Networker' No 465020, arriving at the opposite platform, forms the 15.57 service from Charing Cross to Gillingham via the North Kent Line. *A. E. Bennett/BM*

GRAVESEND: Before the North Kent Line opened to Gravesend in 1849, the town had been served by the 'Long Ferry' steamships from London Bridge, which were recorded in 1830 as carrying a million passengers a year. In the same way as the other principal stations on the line, the Gravesend buildings were constructed to a Samuel Beazley design, but unlike most of the others, this one and the station at Erith still survive. Although electrification was extended to here in 1930, this did not affect the branch-line trains, which remained steam-hauled. On 16 June 1960 a two-coach train from Allhallows arrives at Gravesend Central (as it was then) behind two Wainwright-designed locomotives, Class 'H' 0-4-4T No 31512 leading 'C' Class 0-6-0 No 31510.

Almost exactly 23 years later, on 19 June 1993, the square platform building behind the leading locomotive is no longer in evidence, and the branch traffic has all gone, but little else seems to have changed as Class '415/4' 4EPB No 5431 enters the same platform, leading the 17.48 train to Cannon Street. *John Faulkner/BB*

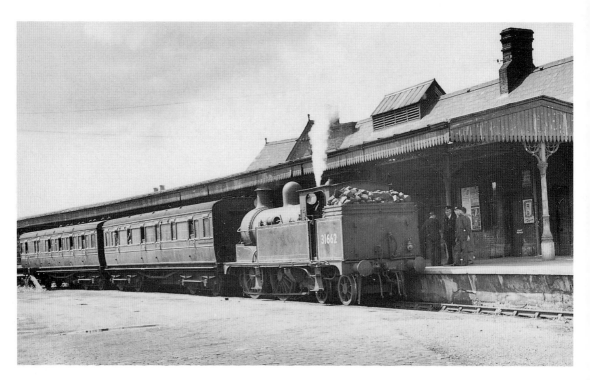

GRAVESEND WEST: The branch line from Fawkham Junction to Gravesend (Gravesend West Street from 1899 and Gravesend West from 1949) was incorporated by the Gravesend Railway and opened by the LC&DR in May 1886. Initially the line enjoyed 14 trains a day, all travelling the 27½ miles from London Victoria. The SER's route from Charing Cross to Gravesend Central, however, was shorter and faster, and there was also opposition from the London, Tilbury & Southend Railway with its cheap services to the Tilbury Ferry on the other side of the Thames. Passenger traffic became light, and in later years was almost entirely local. Services were withdrawn in August 1953, and Gravesend West then continued as a goods depot for another 15 years until the line was truncated at Southfleet, where a coal depot survived for a few more years. Two weeks before passenger trains ceased, 1891 Kirtley-designed Class 'R' 0-4-4T No 31662 is seen at the terminus in company with its two ancient-looking coaches.

Currently the station site awaits development, and is used by a few people as a car park. Just a part of the platform and station wall remain. *R. C. Riley/BM*

ROSHERVILLE: The main reason for construction of the branch to Gravesend West was to provide a fast journey from London to the important leisure resort gardens at Rosherville, previously served only by river craft. Unfortunately, public interest in the gardens was beginning to decline, and they closed completely in 1910; the station eventually became an unstaffed halt, and was closed in 1933. Trains on the line continued to steam past the grass-grown platforms, however, as was the case on 20 September 1952, with 'H' Class 0-4-4T No 31295 hauling the usual two coaches for Farningham Road.

Today the cutting is still in existence, although it now carries lines of traffic on the busy Thames Way road that connects Gravesend with the main A2 trunk route. The skyline has changed but one of the buildings can still be seen to provide a reference point. *J. H. Aston/BM*

GILLINGHAM: Pronounced with a soft 'G', unlike the town of the same name in Dorset, the station of Gillingham, Kent, was first called New Brompton. Dating from 1858, it was originally a country stop on the East Kent Railway's eastern extension from Chatham, but today is a busy commuter station with frequent services direct to both Charing Cross and Victoria. On 30 September 1958 Maunsell 'Schools' Class 4-4-0 No 30908 *Westminster* approaches the station from the east with a train from Ramsgate to Victoria.

Although the sidings on the right are now a staff walkway, and the old goods building has gone together with the footbridge covering, the scene on a foggy 12 February 1993 has changed very little. Of course the semaphore signals are no more, but the houses adjacent to the line are still occupied and the signal box is still a very busy one, as Class '47/3' No 47359 passes with the 13.41 freight from Sheerness to Willesden Brent. *R. C. Riley/BM*

GILLINGHAM SHED (73D): Dating from 1885, the engine shed at Gillingham was originally known by the same name as the station, New Brompton. By May 1959, when the first view was taken, the decorative brickwork and arched entrances had only 13 months left before closure and subsequent demolition.

A depot for maintenance of EMU stock now stands on the same site, and on the same foggy February day as depicted opposite, Class '413/2' 4CAP No 3205 and Class '415/6' 4EPB No 5601 are both evident, together with a Class '466' 'Networker', which can be glimpsed deep inside the building. *R. C. Riley/BM*

19

Hundred of Hoo Railway

HOO JUNCTION: Retaining the picturesque Saxon name for the district, the Hundred of Hoo Railway Company obtained powers in 1879 to construct a line from Hoo Junction to the village of Stoke, and then on to Grain, a distance of 12½ miles. The company was absorbed by the SER in 1881, who went on to extend the route further in 1882 to a pier on the bank of the River Medway, which was given the name Port Victoria after the reigning monarch. After a chequered existence, however, the terminus was closed in 1951, with the line being truncated at Grain. Meanwhile a short branch off the Hundred of Hoo route had opened to Allhallows-on-Sea in May 1932, but this, together with the route to Grain, closed to passengers in December 1961. Headed by 'H' Class 0-4-4T No 31518, the 14.24 train from Allhallows to Gravesend Central comes off the branch on 14 October 1961 and passes the tiny Hoo Junction Staff Halt platform, while a diesel shunter works the yard on the right.

Overall, the scene today has changed very little, although the redundant water columns and semaphore signals are missing, and the overhead catenary for long-withdrawn Class '71' electric locomotives has been replaced by lighting masts. On 20 November 1993 Class '59/1' No 59103 *Village of Mells* passes the same location, hauling the 10.00 ARC train from Allington to Whatley Quarry. *Terry Gough/BM*

CLIFFE: Originally the only intermediate stations on the Hundred of Hoo line were at Cliffe and Sharnal Street, but in 1906 halts were opened at Uralite, High Halstow, Beluncle, Middle Stoke and Grain Crossing. Nothing remains of them today, although the line is still open to Grain for freight traffic. On April Fools' Day 1961 it rather looks as if a trick is being played on seven-month-old Type 3 Bo-Bo diesel No D6521 (later Class '33/1' No 33108), as it is obliged to deputise for the more usual 0-4-4T steam engine, making the stop at Cliffe station coupled to two old LC&DR coaches that form the 13.06 local service from Gravesend Central to Allhallows-on-Sea.

Only the strengthened road bridge remains as a point of reference as Class '47/0' No 47258 passes the station site on 21 January 1994, hauling the 05.53 Freightliner from Crewe Basford Hall to the Thamesport terminal at **Grain.** *John Faulkner/BM*

GRAIN: The oil refineries on the Isle of Grain were considerably enlarged and extended after the end of the Second World War, and additional land on both sides of the railway was taken for the purpose. Both Port Victoria and Grain Halt closed in 1951, and a new terminus at Grain was opened 400 yards east of the halt. The development brought additional freight to the line, but passenger traffic declined as more visitors travelled by road. With the island platform still looking new on 8 July 1957, Class 'H' 0-4-4T No 31512 awaits departure on the right with the 16.49 train to Gravesend Central. Class 'N' 'Mogul' No 31860 uses the other side of the platform as a temporary stabling point, as the crew return after their break to attach the engine to a freight waiting to leave for Hither Green.

Currently, the sidings on both sides of the now overgrown platform remain, and freight now passes through the old station, heading for the new Thamesport Freightliner facility, which has been constructed a short distance further on, beside the Thames Estuary. *John Faulkner/BM*

ALLHALLOWS-ON-SEA: Situated at the end of a 1³/₄-mile branch from the Hundred of Hoo line half a mile east of Middle Stoke Halt, Allhallows-on-Sea opened on 14 May 1932 to serve a new housing estate. Attempts to develop it as a new seaside residential area, however, failed, and through coaches attached to two fast morning trains to London, and corresponding evening return services, were soon withdrawn. After a life of less than 30 years, paucity of travellers resulted in complete closure of the branch on 4 December 1961. On Whitsun Monday, 6 June 1960, however, the station appears quite busy as two trains to Gravesend occupy the grass-grown platform, Class 'C' 0-6-0 No 31510 on the left, and 'H' Class 0-4-4T No 31512 on the right.

The building above the first coach of the train on the left is the 'British Pilot' public house, the only point of reference remaining in 1993, the station site now being occupied by residential caravans. *John Faulkner/BM*

Main line to Folkestone

BECKENHAM JUNCTION: The first Beckenham station was opened by the Mid-Kent Railway on New Year's Day 1857 as the terminus of its line from Lewisham, and became a junction in the following year when the young LC&DR opened its route between Bromley and Bickley to gain access to London in 1860. Although on the main line from Victoria, express workings do not stop at the station, residents of Beckenham being required to travel to Bromley South. Beckenham Junction is well served by local services, however, with four trains every hour from Victoria via either West Dulwich or Crystal Palace. On 17 June 1954 an excursion from Herne Hill to Ramsgate passes through hauled by 'D1' Class 4-4-0 No 31743.

At the same position on 13 June 1993 the 'Orient Express' for Folkestone Harbour passes the multiple aspect signalling which has replaced the elegant semaphore signal gantry, powered by Class '73/2' electro-diesel No 73201 *Broadlands*. *Stanley Creer/BB*

SHORTLANDS: Originally called Bromley, the station here was opened by the West End of London & Crystal Palace Railway in May 1858. It was enlarged in 1892-4, and commuters currently have two 'Thameslink' trains between Sevenoaks and Bedford each hour, together with another half-hourly service between Victoria and Orpington. Main-line services do not stop here, but a variety of such trains pass through, including Channel Tunnel services from 1994. On 23 June 1970 Type 4 1-Co-Co-1 Diesel No D46 (later Class '45/0' No 45037) approaches Shortlands with two brake tenders and a train of coal empties heading for one of the East Midlands collieries.

At the same location, just after dawn on 13 July 1993, a Class '373' 'Eurostar' Channel Tunnel train returns towards London after overnight gauging trials. With half-set No 3001 leading, the rake is not yet under third rail power, and traction is provided by two Class '73/1' electro-diesels, one out of sight on the front and the other bringing up the rear of the train. *BB/BM*

BROMLEY SOUTH: Prior to coming under the auspices of the LC&DR in 1862, the Mid-Kent (Bromley & St Mary Cray) Railway opened its Bromley station in November 1858. Now known as Bromley South, the station today is an important interchange served by both express and suburban services, with a great number of trains calling daily. Leaving the station on 11 September 1960, work-stained rebuilt 'West Country' 'Pacific' No 34022 *Exmoor* hauls all-Southern-green stock for Dover Marine via Maidstone East.

Seen again on 14 August 1993, one of the sidings has been taken out together with the cross-over, and a new road bridge across the station platforms is evident. Restarting the 06.53 Liverpool Lime Street-Dover Western Docks 'InterCity Holidaymaker Express', Class '47/4 'No 47803 bears InterCity Infrastructure yellow and grey livery, and is generally known to enthusiasts as the 'yellow peril'. *D. B. Clark/BB*

BICKLEY: The Mid-Kent Railway line between Shortlands and Southborough Road opened in July 1858. Renamed Bickley in 1860, the station was joined with the LC&DR from Rochester in December of the same year, and with the SER line from Tonbridge in 1902. Currently it enjoys local services exactly the same as those described for Shortlands on page 25. Climbing the 1 in 100 gradient away from the station on 10 November 1957, Class 'O1' 0-6-0 No 31064 heads the 'Kentish Heights Special', a rambler's excursion from the Western Region to Westerham, having taken over the train at Kensington Olympia.

Bickley station's brickwork has received a facelift and the semaphore signals have gone, but otherwise the same view on 21 March 1992 shows little change except for trackwork alterations, as Class '73/1' No 73103 hauls the 06.36 Tonbridge-Ravensbourne-Tonbridge engineer's train, which consists of 25 'Grampus' wagons loaded with ballast. *Stanley Creer/BB*

BICKLEY JUNCTION: With Bickley Junction signal box in the background, Bulleid 'Merchant Navy' 'Pacific' No 35028 *Clan Line*, in unrebuilt form, heads the 'Golden Arrow' for Dover Marine on 7 April 1954, and curves away from the main line and on to the first section of the loop line to Petts Wood Junction, where the main lines from Victoria and Charing Cross are joined. This particular track alignment was radically changed in the late 1950s (see page 51) and for over 30 years this view was nothing more than a filled-in cutting. With the chord (as it is now called) now doubled from two to four tracks for Channel Tunnel traffic, however, large sections of the old alignment have been reinstated, and the view on 12 November 1993 is again comparable as Class '465/0' 'Networker' No 465017 forms the 11.38 train from Victoria to Orpington. *Both BM*

ST MARY CRAY CUTTING: These two views have been included as an illustration of how BR is attempting to cope with its annual autumn leaf fall problem. Rounding the curve between St Mary Cray Junction and St Mary Cray station on 19 May 1982, Class '414/3' 2HAP EMU No 6062 leads another unit of the same type, both in BR 'Corporate blue' livery, to form a semi-fast service from Victoria to Ramsgate via Chatham. The cutting is overgrown, making the rails particularly susceptible to a build-up of the leaf fall mulch that causes wheel-slip, and occasionally results in burnt-out traction motors.

To offset the problem to some extent, the trees and foliage nearest to the tracks have been cut back, and on 25 April 1992 the cutting has a more orderly appearance as Class '33/0' No 33033 passes through with type ZBA 'Carp' ballast hoppers, working an engineer's train back from Bellingham to Hoo Junction. *Both BM*

ST MARY CRAY: The station here was opened by the LC&DR in 1860, and completely rebuilt by BR in the late 1950s. Soon after the rebuilding, 'Battle of Britain' 'Pacific' No 34086 *219 Squadron* hammers through the island platforms on 16 May 1959 with a Victoria-bound 'Continental Express' boat train with passengers from Ostend.

Apart from the increase in foliage, the now modern platform lighting and the absence of the platform shelters are both apparent in this scene of 19 June 1993, as Class '421/4' 4CIG EMU No 1840 restarts the 12.24 Dover Priory-Victoria service. *R. C. Riley/BB*

CHISLEHURST LOOP: This section of line connects the Victoria main line at St Mary Cray with the Charing Cross main line at Chislehurst. Known as the Chislehurst Loop, the short stretch of single track railway was a favourite of photographers in steam days as it was busy, particularly with freight workings, and picturesque from a number of vantage points. Hauling a mixed goods working in May 1959, BR Derby Type 2 Bo-Bo (later Class '24') No D5010 negotiates the loop and heads for Hither Green.

On 26 June 1993 the same scene is scarcely recognisable, and the same camera position is impossible. With attention from the BR vegetation control unit seemingly well overdue, Class '56' No 56031 *Merehead* passes the same location with the 06.45 Hoo Junction-Mottingham engineer's ballast train. *Derek Cross/BM*

MAIDSTONE EAST: Having received authority for its extension to Maidstone East in 1862, the Sevenoaks Railway then changed its name to the Sevenoaks, Maidstone & Tunbridge (sic) Railway. The line eventually arrived at Maidstone East in 1874, became part of the LC&DR five years later, and reached Ashford in 1884. On 28 March 1961 BR Standard Class '4MT' 2-6-4T No 80038 is watered up, having arrived with the 18.09 train from Ashford.

On 30 November 1993 Class '423/0' 4VEP No 3164 departs from the station as the 12.00 from Ashford to Victoria. The opposite platform has been lengthened, a large building has appeared on the right, and the water column, bay platform and signal box have all been removed as victims of modernisation. *Terry Gough/BM*

BEARSTED: When the LC&DR line from Maidstone East to Ashford opened in July 1884, one of the stations constructed on the route was Bearsted & Thurnham. Later becoming plain Bearsted, a train of carflats loaded with Bedford vans from Luton to Shorncliffe passes the signal box there on 23 April 1960, hauled by 'N' Class 'Mogul' No 31403.

By 9 May 1993 the signal box has gone together with the siding, and background foliage is beginning to dominate the scene, as Class '73/2' No 73201 *Broadlands* approaches the station hauling the 12.00 'Orient Express' from Victoria to Victoria. This is a dining special and the passengers are having their lunch served while the train tours Kent. *Stanley Creer/BM*

LENHAM (1): Another 1884 LC&DR station on the line between Maidstone East and Ashford, the original down-side buildings at Lenham still remain. On 28 March 1961 an eastbound mixed freight passes through the platform hauled by Bulleid Class 'Q1' 'Austerity' 0-6-0 No 33033.

By 25 April 1993 a passenger overbridge has appeared, new lighting columns are evident, the canopies have received some paint, the wooden fence with the 'Wright's Coal Tar Soap' advertisement is no more, and the seemingly mandatory NSE platform clock registers 08.38. Just 3 minutes behind time, the 07.04 Victoria-Ashford train, formed of Class '423/0' 4VEP EMU No 3171, makes the scheduled stop. *Terry Gough/BM*

LENHAM (2): With the embankment newly landscaped to allow for the implementation of a new siding, BR Derby Type 2 Bo-Bo diesel (later Class '24') No D5013 restarts from Lenham on 22 April 1961 with a stopping train for Ashford. Giving a clear indication of how land returns to nature, the same location on 25 April 1993 shows the 00.45 Hoo Junction to Tonbridge engineer's train (after an overnight possession at Crayford) powered by two Class '33/0s', No 33029 leading No 33042. The leading locomotive retains BR 'Corporate blue' livery, with the second one sporting Railfreight Construction colours. *Rodney Lissenden/BB*

ASHFORD: The original South Eastern Railway main line reached Ashford in December 1842, and by February 1844 trains were running through the town to Dover. When the route to Margate opened in 1846 Ashford became a junction, and when the line to Hastings opened in 1851 it became an important interchange, with a fourth line built by the LC&DR coming into the town from Maidstone East in 1884. Leaving the station on 23 August 1951, Wainwright 'D' Class 4-4-0 No 31488 hauls a four-coach train for Tonbridge.

Apart from tree branches precluding the exact angle of view being used on the same footbridge on 25 April 1993, the siding has been taken up, the third rail is evident, and industrial buildings have invaded the green fields. Passing is the 12.30 Charing Cross-Margate train, formed of Class '423/0' 4VEP stock (No 3165 on the rear), and Class '56' No 56031 *Merehead*, putting in another appearance hauling the SKAKO train between Hoo Junction and Tonbridge after reversal in Ashford yards. The locomotive carries Civil Engineer's livery of yellow and grey. *R. C. Riley/BM*

ASHFORD SHED (74A): The first engine shed at Ashford was a four-road structure opened by the SER in the 1840s, and formed part of the works complex. The LC&DR built its own two-road shed in 1894, but this was very short-lived, closing at the same time as that company's separate station in 1899. The original shed became increasingly cramped and the Southern Railway constructed a new ten-road depot on the other side of the line in 1931. This building was Classified 74A in 1950 and was in use for 37 years before an unsuccessful attempt was made to use the facility as the Ashford Steam Centre. On 22 May 1954 Class 'O1' 0-6-0 No 31064 is watered up in the shed yard.

On 20 October 1993 the three walls are still standing, together with the old water tower, and the area awaits complete demolition and development. *Both BM*

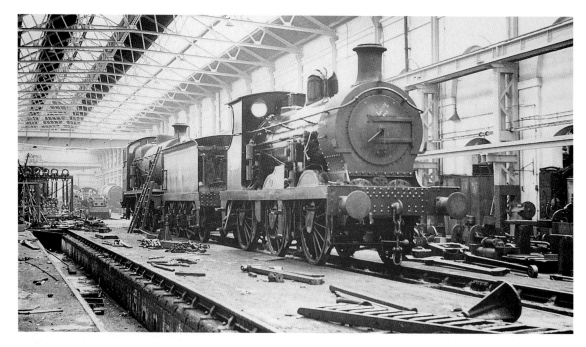

ASHFORD WORKS: The locomotive works built by the SER at Ashford in 1847 covered a 26½-acre site east of the station and was instrumental in Ashford becoming a railway town. Construction of the first locomotive commenced in 1848, and a total of some 639 were completed there up to 1962, when all locomotive work was transferred to Eastleigh. The major site buildings remain today, and although some are in private hands, the erecting shop itself is still in use by BR and is used for repairs and maintenance of Civil Engineer's plant and track machinery. On 22 May 1954 Class 'C' 0-6-0 No 31719 and Class 'K' 'Mogul' No 32347 stand in the position where the administrative building block is situated today. *Both BM*

WILLESBOROUGH: Passing Ashford Works and approaching Willesborough Crossing, just east of Ashford, a summer extra from Victoria to Dover in 1961 is hauled away from the station by 'West Country' 'light Pacific' No 34092 *City of Wells*, a locomotive now preserved at the Keighley & Worth Valley Railway.

As the first 'Eurostar' Class '373' Channel Tunnel test train is hauled from North Pole International Depot to Dollands Moor for trials on 5 November 1993, the two Class '73/1' electro-diesels providing traction, Nos 73107 and 73126 *Kent & East Sussex Railway*, pass the same location. The woodland on the right was the site of the once extensive Ashford shed yards. *Rodney Lissenden/BM*

SANDLING station opened as a junction in 1888 at the point where, from 1874, the branch to Sandgate deviated from the Dover main line. It had been intended that the line to Sandgate should continue for a further 3 miles to Folkestone Harbour, which would have avoided the harbour incline, but the plans came to nothing and the branch was cut back to Hythe in 1931. Sandgate station became a bus garage, and the line to Hythe itself closed in December 1951. A few months prior to the branch services being withdrawn, Class 'H' 0-4-4T No 31521 is in the bay platform with the train for Hythe, as Class 'L1' 4-4-0 No 31789 passes through with a London-bound additional passenger service from Dover.

On 18 November 1993, exactly the same camera position is made impossible by overhanging tree branches, as a pair of Class '423' 4VEP EMUs, Nos 3177 and 3473, call at Sandling forming the 10.16 train from Ramsgate to Charing Cross. The branch platform is no longer in use, the signal box which controlled it has gone, and the Station Master's house, although still in existence, is now completely obscured by the embankment woodland. *R. C. Riley/BM*

HYTHE: The 3½-mile line from the junction where Sandling station is now situated, through Hythe to Sandgate, was completed in 1874. Both stations were high above and remote from the towns that they purported to serve, and plans to connect them with the Folkestone, Hythe & Sandgate horse tramway failed to materialise. The line between Hythe and Sandgate closed in April 1931, and following years of diminishing traffic, the remaining part of the route between Sandling and Hythe followed suit in December 1951. On 28 August 1951 Hythe station looks particularly uncared for, as 'H' Class 0-4-4T No 31521 awaits departure with the auto-train for Sandling Junction.

Today all trace of the site has vanished, this view having been taken from the back garden of a residence which is still named the 'Station Master's House'. *R. C. Riley/BM*

DOLLANDS MOOR: In preparation for the Channel Tunnel, a large site was cleared to the east of Saltwood Tunnel, near Westenhanger, from 1990, and a new long siding was laid from there to the tunnel portals for transportation of the myriad men, machinery and materials that would be needed for the construction. The siding paralleled the main line to what is now known as Continental Junction, and on 16 November 1991 was in use for an engineer's train headed by Class '73/0' No 73001, with Class '20s' Nos 20138 and 20087 on the rear.

By 18 November 1993 the complete 12-road yard had been completed with overhead electrification in place, as ex-Class '416/4' 2HAP EMU No 6401, converted to mobile driver-training school unit No 931001, passes the same location forming a driver-training run from Stewarts Lane to Dover. Dollands Moor is the interface between the Eurotunnel 25kV overhead line system and the NSE 750V dc third rail network. *Both BM*

FOLKESTONE WARREN: Constructed between the seashore and the chalk cliffs, the stretch of main line at Folkestone Warren is situated between Martello and Abbotscliff tunnels, east of Folkestone, and until expensive remedial measures were taken in 1948 was subject to landslips that closed the line on more than one occasion. On 7 May 1951 the 09.36 Sunday train from Charing Cross to Ramsgate passes, formed of all-green coaching stock and hauled by BR Derby Type 2 Bo-Bo diesel No D5014 (later renumbered 24014).

Although 22 years have passed and the siding and telegraph poles have been taken up, the scene could almost be called timeless, as Class '73/2' No 73210 *Selhurst* powers a Victoria to Dover 'Orient Express' at the same location on 30 January 1993. *M. Pope/BM*

FOLKESTONE HARBOUR: Nearly three-quarters of the mile-long Folkestone Harbour branch was constructed at a severe gradient of between 1 in 30 and 1 in 36. Crossing the harbour itself on a series of brick arches and a swing bridge, it opened for goods traffic in 1843 and to passengers on the first day of 1849, although the first station buildings were not completed until 1850. The present station dates from 1853, but it was increased in size on a piecemeal basis on three separate occasions to 1909. Departing from the station in the 1950s with the empty coaching stock of the 'Golden Arrow' from Victoria, and attacking the climb to Folkestone Junction, the pair of Stirling 'R1' Class 0-6-0Ts are from a Class introduced by the SER in 1888; No 31154 is leading No 31069, which has a cut-down cab for negotiating Tyler Hill tunnel on the Whitstable Harbour branch (see page 97), but has later been refitted with a full-height chimney.

Some 40 years later the mode of travel by both rail and sea is rather more commensurate with the present day, but otherwise the scene has changed very little as Class '47/4' No 47565 crosses the harbour with empty stock of the 'Orient Express', which has also emanated from Victoria. *Dr P. Ransome-Wallis/BM*

Marsh Line

HAM STREET: Marketed by NSE as the 'Marsh Line', the Ashford-Hastings route was first conceived by the Brighton, Lewes & Hastings Railway as a means of extending its coastal line to Ashford. However, the project fell to the SER to complete, and that company abandoned its own alternative of a branch to Hastings from Headcorn; the line opened in 1851. The station at Ham Street was renamed Ham Street & Orlestone in 1897 but dropped the Orlestone again in 1976. Climbing the 1 in 100 gradient through the station on 6 August 1961, Class 'C' and 'Q1' Class 0-6-0s Nos 31004 and 33028 head for Ashford with an engineer's train.

At the same position on 1 July 1993 the gas lamp, semaphore signals and siding have all been removed and the trees have grown, but otherwise there is very little change evident as green-liveried Class '33/0' No 33008 *Eastleigh* passes the station with a train of two nuclear flasks from Dungeness to Sellafield. *Dennis Ovenden/BM*

BROOKLAND HALT: Branching off from the Ashford-Hastings line at Appledore, the Lydd Railway route to Dungeness opened in 1881. Another branch south of Lydd (later Lydd Town) then opened to New Romney & Littlestone-on-Sea in 1884. Dungeness terminus closed to passengers in 1937, and trains then terminated at Lydd Town. The halt at Brookland, together with all passenger services on both branches, however, ceased in 1967, although the track to Dungeness still remains open for one booked train per week transporting nuclear flasks between Dungeness Power Station and Sellafield, as illustrated on the previous page. On 28 February 1961 Class 'C' 0-6-0 No 31218 has just passed over the level crossing at Brookland with a train that supplied drinking water to the various crossing-keepers who then operated the manual gates between Appledore and Lydd Town, the water being transported in an ex-SE&CR engine tender next to the brake-van.

The present scene on 13 November 1993 was taken just after a dull dawn and is an engineer's train from Hoo Junction, heading for the site of Lydd Town station where it will run round. Traction is being provided by Class '33/0' No 33063. *M. Edwards/BM*

NEW ROMNEY & LITTLESTONE: Originally a contender for the United Kingdom's longest station name, New Romney & Littlestone-on-Sea terminus opened in June 1884, with the 'on-Sea' being discarded four years later. Passenger services ceased on 6 March 1967, and the only railway now remaining in New Romney is the narrow-gauge Romney, Hythe & Dymchurch Railway, the station building for which can be seen on the extreme right of both scenes, providing the one remaining point of reference. On 10 November 1966 Class '3H' 'Hampshire' diesel-electric multiple unit (DEMU) No 1116 (now Class '205') awaits departure for Ashford. On 25 August 1993 a modern warehouse stands on the station site. *John Vaughan/BB*

RYE: Opening with the Ashford-Hastings line in 1851, Rye is the most important stop on the route, the station retaining a listed building on the Hastings platform which has been described as 'one of the best examples of railway Italianate'. Although threatened with closure on more than one occasion, the line remains open, and may be the subject of future electrification, as an important link for passengers from the South Coast wishing to join Channel Tunnel trains at the forthcoming Ashford International station, without having to travel to London. Passing between the staggered down platform and the signal box on 4 August 1988 a Class '207' DEMU No 207011 forms the 15.05 train from Hastings to Ashford.

With the signal box having been re-tiled and having a new coat of paint, and the trees on the horizon having grown a little, the scene on 6 June 1992 depicts a steam special from Hastings to Ashford, run in connection with the 'Ashford 150' celebrations, and hauled by rebuilt 'West Country' 'Pacific' No 34027 *Taw Valley*. *Both BM*

ORE SHED: Although the SER reached Hastings from Ashford in 1851, the station at Ore did not open until 1888. Its importance was considerably increased in 1935 when, because of limited accommodation at Hastings, electrification was extended to there from the latter, and Ore station was used as a terminus for trains from the west. A four-road service depot for the EMUs was constructed there and on 27 July 1982 contained Class '421/2' 4CIG unit No 7368, which is emerging from the structure to form the 18.22 service from Ore to London Victoria.

When revisited on 13 November 1993 the building and tracks remained but nature was beginning to reclaim the area for its own. The station building on the left has been demolished, and the station itself is now unstaffed. *Both BM*

Main line to Hastings

ELMSTEAD WOODS: The SER shortened its route from London to Tonbridge via Redhill by 12½ miles when it constructed a new cut-off between St Johns and Tonbridge, via Chislehurst and Orpington, which opened for passengers in 1868. A station called Elmstead opened in 1904 and received its present suffix four years later. The tunnels opening out on to the station platforms, however, are still known as Chislehurst Tunnels, so named as the nearest station to the portals when constructed was at Chislehurst, one mile down the line. Displaying the early style of front-end yellow warning panel, a Charing Cross-Hastings train passes through the station on 9 March 1968, formed of Class '6S' 'Hastings' DEMU (later Class '201') No 1001.

By 22 June 1992 foliage between the two pairs of tracks has obliterated a view of the second tunnel portal, the platforms have been lengthened and provided with more up-to-date lighting, and the staff hut on the island platform has been demolished. Passing through at speed, Class '411/5' 4CEP EMUs Nos 1527 and 1545 form the 14.30 Charing Cross-Ramsgate train. *J. H. Cooper-Smith/BM*

PETTS WOOD JUNCTION: Four separate loop lines connect the main Kent Coast route from Victoria with that from Charing Cross. Snaking around the curves of the original alignment between Bickley Junction and Petts Wood Junction on the first day of 1959, four-car non-corridor 4SUB EMU No 4516 approaches Petts Wood forming a local service from Victoria to Orpington. In connection with the first phase of the Kent Coast electrification of the late 1950s, the loop is here in course of being realigned to allow for higher speeds, the finished result illustrated on the cover of this book.

Subsequently, trackwork very near to the original alignment was again brought back into use when the loop was doubled to provide two lines for Channel Tunnel traffic in 1993. From the same position on 8 January 1994, Class '466' and Class '465/2' 'Networkers' Nos 466033 and 465248 form the 13.22 train from Orpington to Victoria. *Rodney Lissenden/BM*

ORPINGTON: The railway arrived at Orpington in 1868 when the SER opened the line from Chislehurst to Tonbridge. The station buildings were modernised and the layout enlarged in 1901, and at the same time the first engine shed there was constructed. This was destined to operate for only a quarter of a century, however, as electrification from 1925 required larger and more modern facilities, and a new four-road maintenance depot was built for the purpose, the original building surviving as offices for Civil Engineering. Passing the EMU depot on 7 February 1989 Class '415/1' 4EPB No 5201 arrives at journey's end as the 12.02 service from Victoria.

In connection with Channel Tunnel traffic, further major engineering works were completed in 1993, resulting in additional station platforms and demolition of the depot. At the same position on 29 October 1993, the 12.07 Dover Priory-Charing Cross train heads away from the camera formed of Class '423/1' 4VEP No 3446. The depot buildings have disappeared and a new footbridge over the lines is evident. *Both BM*

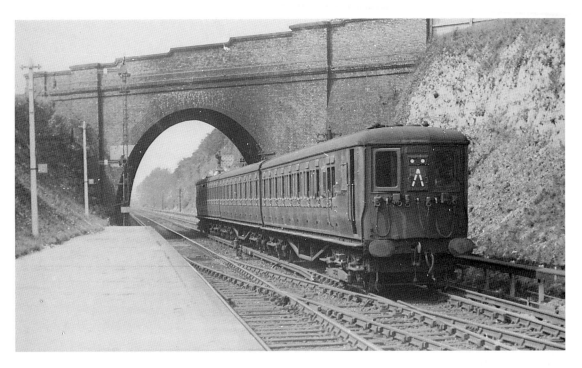

CHELSFIELD: Another station on the 1868 SER cut-off route to Dover via Chislehurst and Tonbridge was Chelsfield, which opened for passengers in March of that year, situated on a gradient of 1 in 120 from east of Orpington to the summit at Knockholt. Entering the station during the mid-1940s, a Charing Cross-Sevenoaks local service is formed of a 3SUB EMU, a type converted from SE&CR steam stock, and passes beneath the distinctive road bridge overlooking the station platforms.

Providing a striking example of how design has changed over the years, modern Class '465/0' 'Networkers' Nos 465031/032 enter the lengthened platform as the 15.00 Charing Cross-Sevenoaks train on 23 October 1993. *John Faulkner collection/BM*

DUNTON GREEN: When this undated print came to hand, it seemed to epitomise the Kent countryside, and it was decided to include it in this book despite the location being noted only as 'passing through the fields of Kent'! The county is quite a large one, but after following a few false trails the location was discovered as a footbridge on the North Downs Way just north of Dunton Green station. It is near to the village of Otford, but not on the same line as Otford station itself. Rebuilt 'West Country' 'light Pacific' No 34004 *Yeovil* heads an express for Dover.

Contrasting with the 'West Country', Class '373' 'Eurostar' sets Nos 3101/3102 form a test train from North Pole International Depot to the Channel Tunnel portals at Cheriton, Folkestone, on 11 February 1994. The telegraph poles have gone, and the 'fields of Kent' are slowly vanishing from view behind a proliferation of greenery, but the location is still a very attractive one. *D. Sellman/BB*

BRASTED: Incorporated by the Westerham Valley Railway in 1876 and opened by the SER in July 1881, the branch from the main line at Dunton Green to Westerham had two halts *en route*, Brasted, which opened with the line, and Chevening, which opened in 1906. Closure came about in 1961, and lengths of the route have since totally disappeared beneath the M25 motorway. Just ten days prior to closure, on 21 October 1961, the usual two-coach push-pull set arrives at Brasted Halt headed by Wainwright 'H' Class 0-4-4T No 31263. At the same spot today, road vehicles pass by ceaselessly on the M25. *John Faulkner/BM*

WESTERHAM: Closure of the Westerham branch in 1961 came as an unpleasant surprise to many people (particularly the 167 regular season ticket holders!) as the order was made by the Government of the day in the face of a recommendation against closure by the Transport Users' Consultative Committee. Probably its length of 4³/₄ miles contrived against survival, as had it been just a little shorter it could have been electrified without the expense of having to install an additional sub-station, and it was this cost that undoubtedly influenced the Southern Region to continue with steam haulage. On Easter Monday 1961 the auto-train from Dunton Green stands at Westerham terminus headed by the usual 'H' Class 0-4-4T, on this occasion No 31324. The site today is taken up by a furniture warehouse. *Stanley Creer/BB*

SEVENOAKS: The main railway route serving Sevenoaks is the SER 'cut-off' completed in 1868 to shorten the company's original route to Dover via Redhill. The station was called Sevenoaks (Tubs Hill), in order to differentiate it from the second route into the town originated by the Sevenoaks Railway's single line from Sevenoaks Junction (now Swanley) to Sevenoaks (Bat & Ball) which had opened in 1862, and joined with the main line in 1869. Today the two stations are known as Sevenoaks and Bat & Ball. Believed to have been the last regular duty for a pre-Grouping SR 4-4-0 in the London area, the 07.24 train from London Bridge to Ramsgate and Deal arrives at Sevenoaks on 28 September 1960 behind Wainwright 'D1' Class No 31749, the train having originated as the 06.56 empty stock working from Holborn Viaduct to London Bridge.

From the same vantage point on 11 November 1993 Class '421/4' 4CIG unit No 1809 leads the 09.40 train from Charing Cross to Hastings. Apart from the more modern signal box, and the obvious trackwork rationalisation that has occurred, the old railway building on the left still survives in private hands, and the electric sub-station beside the lines to Bat & Ball on the right is still apparent. *G. D. King/BM*

HILDENBOROUGH BANK: Always a popular location for photography in steam days, the 1 in 122/144 6-mile rising gradient from Tonbridge to Sevenoaks took its name from the one intermediate station on the section, Hildenborough. The bank provided a tough test for heavy steam-hauled trains, but is of little apparent consequence to modern motive power since completion of the Kent Coast electrification in the early 1960s. On the southern slopes of the bank approaching Hildenborough station on the down grade on 23 May 1953, a Dover-bound 'Continental Express' is powered by BR Standard 'Britannia' 'Pacific' No 70014 *Iron Duke*.

At the same location on 26 January 1994 Class '421/4' 4CIG No 1871 heads the 11.10 Charing Cross-Hastings service. *Both BM*

HILDENBOROUGH station dates from the opening of the SER 'cut-off' route and opened to passengers on 1 May 1868. One of the many 'H' Class 0-4-4Ts allocated to Tonbridge shed for local services in Kent, No 31164, enters the station on 23 May 1953, hauling the 17.05 local service from Tonbridge to Dunton Green.

On 21 June 1993 a Folkestone Harbour to Victoria boat train rushes past the same spot formed of Class '411/5' 4CEP stock with No 1528 leading. Although the signal box is long gone, third rail has been laid and the platform lengthened, the distinctive tree on the opposite platform appears little different and is still surviving despite the more than 40 years that separates the two scenes. *Both BM*

TONBRIDGE (1): The SER's developing main line reached Tunbridge (as it was then spelt) in 1842, and continued on to Dover, which was reached two years later. The line to Hastings via Tunbridge Wells was completed in 1852, and when the shorter route from London via Chislehurst also arrived in 1868, this completed the Tonbridge railway network and established its importance as a major junction. Approaching the station on 28 September 1960, a stopping train from Ashford is hauled by Maunsell 'Schools' Class 4-4-0 No 30934 *St Lawrence*.

At the same location on 11 November 1993 the 09.16 Ramsgate-Charing Cross service is formed of Class '411/5' 4CEP units Nos 1591/1581. The permanent way here has recently been upgraded to serve as the main route for Channel Tunnel traffic, and although most of the old infrastructure has been swept away, the lineside hut on the right, which was under construction in 1960, still remains, together with a number of the houses in the background. *G. D. King/BM*

TONBRIDGE (2): The photographs on the previous page were taken from the road bridge which can be seen in the background of these scenes, which were recorded over 40 years apart. On 25 July 1953 a Charing Cross-Folkestone train is restarted from Tonbridge station by 'D1' Class 4-4-0 No 31489.

With Class '414/3' 2HAP EMU No 4308 running as empty stock to Ramsgate depot, and passing Class '73/1' No 73105 at the same spot on 11 November 1993, many of the changes of time are apparent, although the bridge and station building above look much the same, if cleaner, and the gabled building in the extreme right background still overlooks the railway. *Stanley Creer/BM*

TONBRIDGE SHED (74D): The SER engine shed at Tonbridge dated from May 1842, and discounting two earlier sheds built for absorbed companies, was the SER's first such depot. Sited in the fork of the Ashford and (later) Hastings lines, the original three-road structure was enlarged in the 1880s, with a number of improvements following over the years, including new brick-screened, steel and asbestos roofs applied by BR in the early 1950s. Classified 74D under Ashford by BR, it was recoded 73J under Stewarts Lane in October 1958 and was eventually downgraded to a Stewarts Lane sub-shed, and then a Redhill (75B) sub-shed after Stewarts Lane closed in September 1963. The shed's remaining locomotive allocation was transferred to Tunbridge Wells West in January 1965, and nothing of the buildings now remains, the site between the lines being occupied by BR Civil Engineers. Locomotives on shed on 26 March 1953 included Kirtley 'R1' Class 0-4-4T No 31704, Billinton 'E4' Class 0-6-2T No 32488 and Wainwright 'C' Class 0-6-0 No 31480. Occupying the same position in November 1993 was a very large rubbish skip. *Both BM*

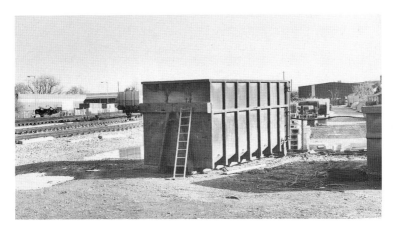

EDENBRIDGE: The original SER main line to Dover via Redhill was opened as far as Ashford by the end of 1842, the station at Edenbridge opening with the stretch of line to Tonbridge on 26 May of that year. Passing through the station in May 1959 'Schools' Class 4-4-0 No 30937 *Epsom* is unsuitably rostered for the 15.18 Redhill-Tonbridge goods train, while a ballast train headed by a Maunsell 'Mogul' awaits an exit from the refuge siding.

The signal gantry used by the photographer is no longer there, and the same elevation was no longer available to record the view from the same position on 9 May 1993 of the 09.55 Redhill-Tonbridge train, formed of Pressed Steel Company Class '117' DMU No L405 with driving motor car No 51381 leading. Third rail is now in situ for electric services in 1994, the semaphore signals are no longer in evidence and the station itself now sports a footbridge. *Derek Cross/BM*

PENSHURST: Situated in the village of Chiddingstone Causeway, some 2 miles north of the town of Penshurst, the station of this name was another of the original stations built by the SER on its first Kent Coast main line in 1842. Subsequently rebuilt, the platforms today contain bus-shelter-style accommodation and the passengers enjoy an hourly service of Redhill-Tonbridge trains, although this could improve following electrification in 1994. With the station buildings still in evidence in the background, BR Standard Class '4MT' 2-6-4T No 80035 restarts its Tonbridge-Redhill train after the Penshurst stop on 4 November 1961.

The 08.50 Tonbridge-Redhill service on 9 May 1993 was provided by the same DMU as depicted opposite, although now the driving motor brake No 51340 faces the camera. The siding has been taken up, the semaphore signal has been replaced by a multiple-aspect colour light, and a footbridge between the platforms has been constructed. *S. C. Nash/BM*

TUNBRIDGE WELLS CENTRAL: The present station at Tunbridge Wells (the appendage 'Central' was dropped after the closure of Tunbridge Wells West) was opened in November 1846, although the town was reached by the SER 14 months earlier when a temporary station at Jackwood Springs was used until tunnel access to the present station was ready for use. The line through to Hastings was finally opened in 1852, and by this time the Brighton, Uckfield & Tunbridge Wells Railway and the East Grinstead, Groombridge & Tunbridge Wells Railway were in operation and opened their branch lines to the town under the auspices of the LB&SCR. One of the Tunbridge Wells West-allocated Drummond 'M7' Class 0-4-4Ts, No 30054, stands in Tunbridge Wells Central platform on 6 August 1956, a particularly unseasonal summer day - there is snow on the ground! - with the 17.23 local service from Tonbridge to Oxted.

On 25 September 1993 the 13.10 train from Charing Cross to Hastings arrives at the same Tunbridge Wells platform formed of Class '423/1' 4VEP unit No 3450. Apart from the removal of some of the London-side platform canopy and the advent of electrification, little change of any significance appears to have taken place over the intervening years. *S. C. Nash/BM*

TUNBRIDGE WELLS WEST: This 1866 station used to boast substantial LB&SCR services from London and Brighton as well as Three Bridges and Eastbourne, but these slowly contracted over the years until all that was left was an hourly Tonbridge-Eridge train. Despite a High Court bid by campaigners to obtain an injunction against closure, BR pulled the plug on the stations of both Tunbridge Wells West and Groombridge and the line between Grove Junction and Birchden Junction on 5 July 1985. The section from Eridge to Tunbridge Wells West has subsequently been taken over by the Tunbridge Wells & Eridge Railway Preservation Society (TWERPS) who eventually hope to operate some services again. With the fine station building showing signs of being run down, the 16.34 train from Eridge to Tonbridge calls on 6 May 1980 formed of Class '207' DEMU No 1301, with fellow unit No 1318 in the yard.

Currently labelled as 'The Old West Station', the building is now a restaurant, and the remainder of the large station complex has been taken over by a Sainsburys supermarket. *Both BM*

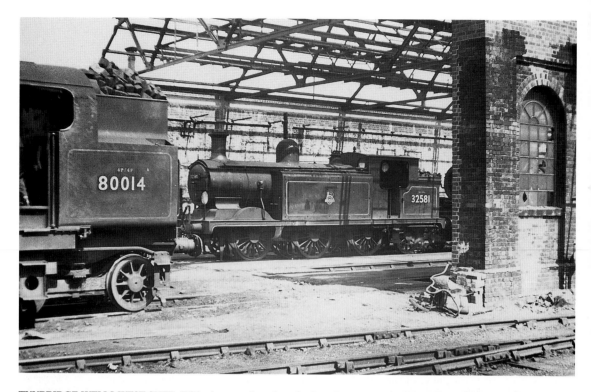

TUNBRIDGE WELLS WEST SHED (75F): A second engine shed at the west end of Tunbridge Wells West station was built in 1890/1, and replaced a two-road shed constructed to the south of the station by the East Grinstead, Groombridge & Tunbridge Wells Railway in 1866. The depot was classified 75F under Brighton by BR and was reduced to a Brighton sub-shed from 1965 when the locomotive allocation was transferred to Brighton and Three Bridges. After Brighton shed closed in 1964, the shed became a sub of Redhill (75B), until final closure in June 1965. The building itself remained, however, to house one of BR's Emergency Control Trains, until that too was declared redundant. The structure is currently empty, but one day may again house working steam under the auspices of the ambitious TWERPS. These two views of the building were recorded on 1 September 1955 and 25 September 1993, the former showing 'E4' Class 0-6-2T No 32581 and BR Standard Class '4MT' 2-6-4T No 80014 in residence. *Terry Gough/BM*

GROOMBRIDGE JUNCTION: The station of Groombridge dated from the opening of the East Grinstead, Groombridge & Tunbridge Wells Railway in October 1866, and was once a busy interchange point, handling traffic from Tunbridge Wells to East Grinstead High Level, to Oxted via Edenbridge Town, and to the south coast at Eastbourne via the Cuckoo Line. On 3 October 1953 ex-LB&SCR Billinton Class 'E4' 0-6-2T No 32582 passes the junction hauling a Tunbridge Wells West to Oxted train.

Currently the junction itself is no more, and the track between Tunbridge Wells West via Groombridge to Eridge is in the hands of TWERPS, who are working towards restoration of services. Some of the society members push a trolley past the same spot on 23 May 1993. *Stanley Creer/BM*

HARTFIELD: The three stations of the single track East Grinstead, Groombridge & Tunbridge Wells Railway opened between East Grinstead and Groombridge in October 1866 were Forest Row, Hartfield and Withyham, the line east of Groombridge to Tunbridge Wells belonging to the Brighton, Uckfield & Tunbridge Wells company. Marketed by the LB&SCR as the 'Pleasant Route', services eventually ceased in January 1967 and the line was taken up. Calling at Hartfield on 3 July 1965 Class '3H' 'Hampshire' DEMU No 1113 forms a Tunbridge Wells West-Three Bridges train.

The old Hartfield station building is now in use as the 'Hartfield Playschool', and the adjoining Station Master's house is a private residence which has been extended and still incorporates the original decorative gable. Just above the hedge can be seen the top of the platform canopy which has been retained by the occupiers as a covered verandah. *J. H. W. Kent/BM*

ETCHINGHAM station opened with the first section of the Hastings line in September 1851, and was constructed on the site of an old manor house. Passing over the level crossing and through the staggered southbound platform on 26 July 1953, Maunsell 'U1' Class 'Mogul' No 31901 heads a London-bound summer special from Hastings.

On 29 December 1993 the 09.52 Hastings-Charing Cross train is rostered for Class '411/5' 4CEP No 1605, which passes the same position at speed, not being required to make the Etchingham stop. The siding, platform canopy, 'Gentlemen' and house in the background have all disappeared - and the weather has decidedly worsened! *R. C. Riley/BB*

CROWHURST: Situated on the climb of up to 1 in 100 from Bopeep Junction to Battle, and a little way from the village of Crowhurst, it is unlikely that a station here would have been built at all had not the LB&SCR constructed Bexhill Central in 1901. The SE&CR thus felt obliged to respond with its own station at Bexhill West, and this was fed as a branch line from Crowhurst in the following year. On a sunny May day in 1957, Class '6L' 'Hastings' DEMU (later Class '202') No 1015 makes the scheduled station stop, the branch auto-train for Bexhill West providing a connection in the bay opposite.

Today a number of Charing Cross-Hastings services still make the Crowhurst stop, as with Class '423/1' 4VEP No 3424 on 8 January 1993. However, there are no longer any services to Bexhill West, and the bay platform has been filled in and the centre roads taken out. With the station buildings demolished, this location is now particularly bleak and unwelcoming. *Michael E. Ware/BM*

Past and Present Colour

Kent and East Sussex

BICKLEY: On a sunny 5 August 1957 two trains heading for the Kent coast pass Bickley station, both hauled by Maunsell-designed engines. Usually powered by a Bulleid 'Pacific', the 'Kentish Belle' Pullman from Victoria to Ramsgate is, on this occasion, entrusted to 'King Arthur' Class 4-6-0 No 30767 *Sir Valence*, the excursion being headed by work-stained Class 'N' 'Mogul' No 31404.

In an attempt to obtain two trains in similar positions, nearly two hours was spent at the same location on 8 January 1994, but luck did not prevail, and in the end it was necessary to make do with a single Class '423/1' 4VEP EMU, No 3446, which is proceeding away from the camera and running as the 13.00 service from Ashford to Victoria. The order of the 'up' and 'down' running lines here has been altered, and the signal box with its attendant semaphore signals has gone together with the telegraph poles; the position of the crossover lines has been moved, and the large tree on the right appears to have died. The change in nature's colours between summer and winter is also readily apparent. *R. C. Riley/Brian Morrison*

ST MARY CRAY: Soon after the two-track section of the line at this location had been doubled, BR Standard Class '5MT' 4-6-0 No 73083 *Pendragon* passes through the newly created cutting near St Mary Cray on 18 May 1959, hauling a train from Ramsgate to Victoria.

In the summer months it is now impossible to duplicate the position from which this photograph was taken, but on 13 March 1994 the tree branches are still devoid of leaves, and allow a view of Class '423/1' 4VEP No 3451 passing the same spot and forming a Sunday train from Margate to Victoria, rescheduled as a result of weekend engineering works. Apart from the absence of semaphore signalling, the concrete cutting walls have discoloured over the years, and the banking is almost unrecognisable. *R. C. Riley/Brian Morrison*

ST MARY CRAY JUNCTION: With the third rail electric current obviously switched off, track maintenance men (then still known as gangers) await the passing of a summer additional working from Victoria to Hastings on 16 May 1959, hauled by 'Schools' Class 4-4-0 No 30937 *Epsom*.

Seen from the same footbridge on 15 January 1994 Class '319/0' 'Thameslink' EMU No 319024 forms the 08.33 train from Bedford to Sevenoaks. The colour change from summer to winter is again self-evident, as is the complete obliteration of the banking on the left by trees and bushes. *R. C. Riley/Brian Morrison*

TONBRIDGE SHED: On the day before the official end of main-line steam operation to the Kent coast, on 12 June 1961, the engine shed of Tonbridge (then designated 73J) contained (from left to right) a Bulleid 'Q1' Class 0-6-0, ex-works Class 'L1' 4-4-0 No 31786, Class 'N1' 'Mogul' No 31877, Class 'N' 'Mogul' No 31871, 0-6-0 diesel shunter No D3044 (later Class '08' No 08032), another Wainwright 'Mogul', and another 0-6-0 diesel shunter, Class '12' No 15220.

Currently nothing remains of the shed, the site being occupied as a storage place for BR Civil Engineer's tools and accoutrements. The Hastings line on the right is all that remains as a point of reference between the two scenes, the present one being photographed on 26 January 1994. *R. C. Riley/Brian Morrison*

ASHFORD: With BR Standard Class '4MT' 2-6-4T No 80065 shunting in the background, the 07.24 train from London Bridge to Ramsgate makes the scheduled stop at Ashford station on 14 May 1960 headed by Class 'D1' 4-4-0 No 31489.

With station improvements under way on 13 March 1994, an equivalent service from Charing Cross to Ramsgate was formed by Class '411/5' 4CEP No 1572. *R. C. Riley/Brian Beer*

RAMSGATE: Shunting empty coaching stock at Ramsgate, Class'C' 0-6-0 No 31245 runs alongside Ramsgate shed (then designated 73G) on 28 March 1959.

The shed was closed to steam later the same year and converted to maintain EMU stock. The original building outline has been maintained for the EMU depot, but there has been extensive remodelling, with the walls now brick-clad and new-style windows incorporated. On 6 March 1994 a Class '421' 4CIG is stabled outside the depot on the same track, as Class '411/5' 4CEP No 1524 travels under the same bridge, departing from the station at the rear of the 15.45 service to Charing Cross. The switched-on headlight is a staff oversight! *R. C. Riley/Brian Morrison*

SHEPHERDS WELL: Hauling a four-coach train from Faversham to Dover, Wainwright Class 'L' 4-4-0 No 31768 slows for the Shepherds Well stop on 23 March 1959.

In the same position on 6 March 1994 Class '411/5' 4CEP No 1552 forms the 12.41 train from Victoria to Dover Western Docks. Although the signal box is still operational, the goods shed, semaphore signal and siding on the right have all become victims of the passing years. A lorry replaces the Morris Minor car in the car park, the 'Southern' station sign has been replaced with a NSE type, and the trees have grown upwards to some extent. The two boys are not thought to be related! *R. C. Riley/Brian Beer*

NEWHAVEN TOWN: Approaching Newhaven Town station and passing the signal box of the same name, a Railway Correspondence & Travel Society special train of 7 October 1962 is hauled over the gated level crossing by 'A1X' Class 'Terrier' 0-6-0T No 32636 piloting Class 'E6' 0-6-2T No 32418.

Now in NSE guise, the signal box still exists to operate what is now a barrier crossing controlling the widened road, although a new road bridge scars the scene to take the majority of traffic over the line to avoid the crossing. With the old telegraph poles and attendant wiring no longer in evidence, the 10.43 train from Brighton to Seaford slows for the station stop on 13 March 1994, formed of Class '421/4' 4CIG No 1855. *R. C. Riley/Brian Morrison*

ST LEONARDS (WEST MARINA): The LB&SCR reached Hastings in 1846 by means of the Brighton, Lewes & Hastings Railway route to St Leonards (Bulverhythe). This became the first St Leonards (West Marina) station, but was closed in 1882 and replaced by a second station of the same name which closed in 1967. On 31 May 1953 a return excursion from Hastings to Tring is hauled through the station by Willesden (1A)-allocated Stanier 'Black Five' 4-6-0 No 45404.

The same scene on 15 November 1993 depicts Class '421/3' 4CIG No 1709 passing the derelict platform and forming the 11.28 service from Hastings to Victoria. *S. C. Nash/BM*

ST LEONARDS SHED (74E): Known as 'Hastings' by the LB&SCR, the shed at St Leonards dated from *circa* 1870, but some form of locomotive facility would have been provided here from the coming of the Brighton, Lewes & Hastings Railway in 1846, as St Leonards (Bulverhythe) was the end of the line until the Bopeep tunnel bore was completed, allowing the company access to the Hastings shed of the SER. The original two-road building here was replaced by a four-road one on virtually the same site, and apart from re-roofing by the SR in 1949, it then remained virtually unchanged until closure in June 1958; the bulk of the shed allocation moved to Ashford, Brighton, Tonbridge and Tunbridge Wells West. Locomotives on depot on 14 August 1956 include Wainwright 'L' Class 4-4-0 No 31762 and two Bulleid 'Q1' 'Austerity' 0-6-0s, No 33032 and No 33039.

The site today is taken up by a carriage washer. On 15 November 1993 Class '411/5' 4CEP No 1550 passes through at the head of empty stock from a Charing Cross-Hastings arrival which is proceeding to St Leonards carriage sidings. *Terry Gough/BM*

HASTINGS: The LB&SCR reached the Hastings area by means of the Brighton, Lewes & Hastings company's 1846 route to St Leonards (Bulverhythe), and the SER arrived by the route from Ashford to Bopeep Junction. A desire by both companies to secure the Hastings business exclusively for themselves resulted in direct confrontation between the rivals on the opening day in February 1851, and matters were not resolved until after High Court proceedings the following year. Amalgamation into the SR finally put paid to any remaining vestiges of the hostility, and the station itself was rebuilt in 1931. Heading a special empty stock working to Polegate, BR Standard Class '4MT' 2-6-4T No 80032 departs from Hastings on 7 September 1963.

From the same vantage point on a very wet 13 November 1993, Class '421/3' 4CIG unit No 1745 begins its journey, forming the 14.28 train to London Victoria. The sidings have been removed and some trees have sprung up, but otherwise the surroundings seem to have changed very little in 30 years. *S. C. Nash/BM*

The Thanet Way

KINGSFERRY BRIDGE, SWALE: Authorised as a replacement to the previously tedious road and ferry route, the Sheerness-on-Sea branch from Sittingbourne was opened by the Sittingbourne & Sheerness Railway in July 1860, the company becoming part of the LC&DR in 1866. The major feature of the line was an Admiralty-designed lifting bridge constructed over the River Swale which connected the Isle of Sheppey with the mainland. In 1906 this was replaced by the SE&CR with a new bridge designed by Sir William Arrol & Company, the firm that designed the famous Forth Bridge and also the current bridge at Swale which was completed in 1959. With the new Kingsferry Bridge under construction on the left, 'C' Class 0-6-0 No 31037 crosses the 1909 structure on 1 May 1959 with a Sheerness-on-Sea to Sittingbourne train.

On 6 February 1993 Class '411/5' 4CEP No 1573 crosses the River Swale forming the 12.27 service from Sheerness-on-Sea to Sittingbourne. All vestiges of the old bridge have disappeared.
Stanley Creer/BM

SHEERNESS-ON-SEA: The first station at Sheerness was opened by the Sittingbourne & Sheerness Railway in July 1860, and services were operated by the LC&DR. A half-mile extension to Sheerness-on-Sea was opened in June 1883, and in time the original station became a goods depot; it was formally closed to passengers in 1922, and to freight in 1963. Departing from Sheerness-on-Sea on 25 May 1958, the 18.33 train for Sittingbourne is hauled by Ivatt Class 2MT 'Mickey Mouse' 2-6-2T No 41309, with 'D1' Class 4-4-0 No 31743 in the background occupying the only platform currently still in use.

On 20 November 1993 the shuttle to Sittingbourne is formed of Class '411/4' 3CEP No 1406. The building in the background, inscribed on the brickwork as the 'Sheerness Economical & Industrial Society Ltd', still stands, but the signal box, semaphore signal and third track no longer exist. *S. C. Nash/BM*

SITTINGBOURNE: Situated on the East Kent Railway's route from Chatham to Canterbury, the station at Sittingbourne opened with the completion of the first section of line constructed between Chatham and Faversham in January 1858. Two years later it became a junction when the Sittingbourne & Sheerness Railway opened its line on to the Isle of Sheppey. Passing the recently extended station platform at Sittingbourne on 30 September 1958, 'D1' Class 4-4-0 No 31739 hauls two vans eastwards to Faversham.

With the siding and goods shed removed, and the platform end having weathered to blend in with the rest of the surroundings, the 12.00 Victoria-Ramsgate 'Orient Express' glides past the same spot on 6 February 1993, powered by Class '73/2' electro-diesel No 73203. *R. C. Riley/BM*

FAVERSHAM: The East Kent Railway line into Faversham opened in January 1858, and became a part of the LC&DR from August of the following year. On the penultimate day of steam working, Saturday 13 June 1959, the 17.52 express from Ramsgate passes Faversham engine shed (73E) in the distance and approaches the station behind 'West Country' 'Pacific' No 34001 *Exeter*.

Apart from an extended platform and a foot crossing having been provided for access to the carriage sidings, little appears to have changed by 7 August 1993, as Class '47/4' No 47824 is seen in the same position with the 13.43 'InterCity Holidaymaker' train from Dover Western Docks to Liverpool Lime Street. The old engine shed building can still be seen in the background behind the train, although it was officially closed in 1959. *R. C. Riley/BM*

SELLING: Situated deep in the fruit country between Faversham and Canterbury East, a station at Selling was added to the Dover main line by the LC&DR in December 1860. Currently only the Victoria-Dover Priory semi-fast trains stop here, and apart from platform extensions, not much appears to have altered since the days of steam, with signal box and attendant semaphore signals still evident. Blasting up the 1 in 100 gradient through the station, 'Battle of Britain' 'Pacific' No 34087 *145 Squadron* hauls the 09.00 Victoria-Dover Marine express on 12 January 1958.

Slowing for the scheduled station stop on 9 April 1993 is Class '423/0' 4VEP No 3185 forming the 07.41 service from Victoria to Dover. *J. Head/BB*

HARBLEDOWN is the point where the main line to Dover through Canterbury East passes over the Ashford-Ramsgate route between Chartham and Canterbury West. Before the trappings of the newly nationalised British Railways had begun to show on the motive power, Class 'C' 0-6-0 No 1291, with 'Southern'-style number and lettering, passes beneath the main line at Harbledown on a summer day in 1948, hauling the 11.40 train from Margate to Ashford.

At the same location on 20 November 1993 the railway boundary appears to have altered, as the fencing at the bottom of the embankment has been replaced by railings much nearer to the line. Also what appears to be a sloping allotment of cabbages in 1948 is now rough pasture. Passing is Class '411/5' 4CEP No 1534, forming the 13.28 train from Margate to Charing Cross. *Rodney Lissenden collection/BM*

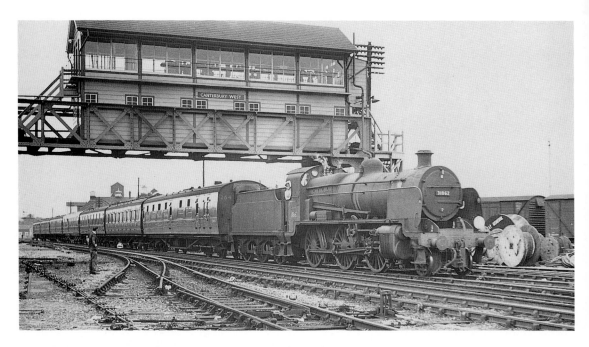

CANTERBURY WEST, one of the two remaining Canterbury stations, and known as plain Canterbury until 1899, was reached from Ashford by the SER in February 1846, and linked to Ramsgate in April of the same year. Probably the most striking feature at the location is the 1928 SE&CR gantry signal box that straddles the tracks. On 25 August 1960 Class 'N' 'Mogul' No 31862 makes its way beneath the structure on arrival with the 10.12 train from Margate to Charing Cross.

With the signal box still appearing to be in fine condition with a fairly recent coat of paint, the 13.28 train from Margate to Charing Cross enters the station on 18 December 1993, formed of Class '423/0' 4VEP No 3183. Newly constructed buildings on both sides of the lines, together with a modern speed restriction disc, do nothing to enhance the view. *Terry Gough/BB*

CANTERBURY EAST, the junior of the two remaining stations at Canterbury by 14 years, was the second station called Canterbury and was opened by the LC&DR in July 1860, the East Kent Railway having changed its name accordingly the year before. Renamed Canterbury East in 1899, the station is served by Victoria-Dover trains, with West station having services between Charing Cross and Margate/Ramsgate. On 13 June 1959, the penultimate day of steam working, begrimed 'C' Class 0-6-0 No 31583 departs from Canterbury East with the 17.12 train from Faversham to Dover Priory.

At the same place on 18 December 1993 Class '423/1' 4VEP unit No 3421 forms the 11.35 train from Victoria to Dover Western Docks. The signal gantry bears one less signal, the siding has been fenced off as a BR staff car park, and the station building has lost one chimney stack and six chimney pots. But at least it still survives, together with the signal box and the old goods shed in the background. *S. C. Nash/BM*

SHEPHERDS WELL (1): Situated nearly at the summit of the long varying gradients from Canterbury in the west and from Dover in the east, the station at Shepherds Well dates from the LC&DR's achievement of a through route from London to Dover, opened in July 1861. It became a junction from 1912, when a line was opened by the East Kent (Light) Railway for coal traffic, transport for both passenger and goods following in 1916. Coming off the junction on to the main line through Shepherds Well station on 6 May 1960, a coal train from Tilmanstone Colliery to Dover is hauled by tender-first '01' Class 0-6-0 No 31258.

On 11 July 1992 InterCity's cross-country 06.44 Liverpool Lime Street-Dover Western Docks train passes through the station platforms powered by Class '47/4' No 47811. Although the railway surroundings have remained basically unaltered over the years, the station building itself has lost part of its structure and the goods shed behind it has been demolished. The London-bound platform shelter still survives together with the signal box, but the semaphore signal has been replaced with a 'colour lights'. The NSE station clock times the passing at 13.04. *Derek Cross/BB*

SHEPHERDS WELL (2): The East Kent (Light) Railway was one of a number of independent lines operated by the legendary Colonel H. F. Stephens from his offices in Tonbridge (another one being the Kent & East Sussex Railway). He obtained a Light Railway Order in 1911 for a line from Shepherds Well to Wingham Colliery, and this opened for coal traffic in 1912. A connection to Tilmanstone Colliery was made in 1916, and in the same year limited passenger services commenced from Shepherds Well (EKR) to Eastry Junction, from where the lines diverged to both Wingham and Sandwich Road, where the route was later extended to the port of Richborough. The anticipated coal exports failed to develop, however, and the extension lay derelict from 1939. Passenger trains on the extension to Sandwich Road had ceased in 1928, and the complete system closed for passengers in 1948, some 10 months after nationalisation. The section from Tilmanstone Colliery to Shepherds Well remained open for coal trains until the miners' strike of 1984. On 6 May 1960 Class 'O1' 0-6-0 No 31065 stands at the old Shepherds Well (EKR) platform with a haul of empty wagons for Tilmanstone Colliery, while diesel shunter No D3044 (later Class '08' No 08032) brings a coal train from Tilmanstone down the branch and approaches the main line.

The site is now in the hands of the East Kent Railway Preservation Society, and on 4 July 1992 the same platform is occupied by preserved vehicles, including the experimental Leyland bus body on bogies, two fruit vans, and Class '08' shunter No 08108. *Derek Cross/BM*

Left DOVER PRIORY: The railway first arrived at Dover in 1844, the SER providing six trains a day each way between London and Dover Town station, which closed in 1914. Dover Priory station was opened by the LC&DR in 1861, taking its name from the nearby ruins of St Martin's Priory. Heading a London-bound special relief, Maunsell 'Schools' Class 4-4-0 No 30938 *St Olave's* emerges from Priory tunnel into Priory station on 24 September 1955.

In the same position on 26 June 1993 a railtour charter from Derby enters the station hauled by Railfreight Petroleum Sector Class '47/0' No 47224. The platforms have been extended, and 'colour light' signals have replaced the semaphore. Above the tunnel the foliage has increased, and the old houses of some character have been replaced by modern brick 'boxes'. *Both BM*

Above DOVER SHED (74C): The five-road engine shed at Dover Marine was constructed by the Southern Railway, and opened in 1928 on reclaimed land to replace the LC&DR shed at Dover Priory, which dated from 1861. The shed was in the front line during the Second World War, being closed for a time after German shelling of the port. It survived hostilities, however, but not the advent of electrification, closure taking place in 1961. Passing the shed on 23 May 1959, BR Standard '5MT' 4-6-0 No 73083 *Pendragon* approaches Dover Marine with empty coaching stock to form a train for Victoria. On the shed can be seen two 'N' Class 'Moguls' and an 'E1' Class 4-4-0, all looking decidedly grubby.

Although Archcliffe Junction signal box survives, no trace of the shed now remains, the site being taken over by part of Dover Town yard. Approaching on 18 December 1993, '09' Class shunter No 09011 hauls a rake of continental 'Ferrywaggons' for the SNCF Ferry at Dover Western Docks. *R. C. Riley/BM*

DOVER WESTERN DOCKS: Trains from Dover Town station to Dover Harbour commenced in November 1861, and subsequently ran on to the pier, Harbour station being replaced by Dover Town & Harbour in 1863. After widening of the pier, Dover Marine station was opened for military traffic in 1915, and to the public after the First World War in 1919. Town & Harbour station closed in 1927, and Dover Marine was renamed Dover Western Docks in 1979. Shunting outside the covered terminus on 4 May 1959 is 'O1' Class 0-6-0 No 31434.

On 18 December 1993 Class '411/5' 4CEP No 1570 departs from the station heading the 09.45 boat train for London Victoria. The stone-arched entrance to the station remains, together with one now electrified track. The platform has been extended and a canopy built, but the station approaches generally have an uncared-for appearance, which may have something to do with the impending closure of the station once Channel Tunnel traffic is fully in operation. *Stanley Creer/BM*

MINSTER station dates from 1846 when the SER line from Ashford to Margate Sands opened, and it became a junction the following year when the route south along the coast to Sandwich and Deal was brought into use. The station was given the title Minster Junction in 1852, and to avoid confusion with Minster station on the Isle of Sheppey, which opened in 1901, was thereafter known as Minster Junction (Thanet). Although the Sheppey station at Minster was renamed Minster-on-Sea in 1906, the 'Thanet' epithet was retained here, although the 'Junction' title was dropped in 1945, the station becoming Minster (Thanet). Minster-on-Sea station closed in 1950, but the 'Thanet' was still not dropped from the other remaining Minster station until 1970, when at last the station became plain Minster once again. On 25 August 1960 an engineer's train enters the London-bound platform hauled by ex-LB&SCR Billinton Class 'K' 'Mogul' No 32340.

Currently the rather austere-looking station has the formerly staggered platforms paralleled, a new footbridge, new houses built on the old railway property, and the platform buildings replaced by a 'bus shelter'. Running into the station on 9 May 1993, a Margate-Charing Cross train is formed of Class '423' 4VEP units Nos 3492 and 3184. *Terry Gough/BB*

RAMSGATE: Although the SER reached Ramsgate from Ashford in 1846, followed by what was to become the LC&DR from the Margate direction in 1863, the present through Ramsgate station dates only from 1926; it was opened by the Southern Railway after completion of a loop line constructed between Broadstairs Junction and St Lawrence Junction, after which both the SER's Ramsgate Town and the LC&DR's Ramsgate Harbour termini were closed. Obscured by the exhaust from 'Schools' Class 4-4-0 No 30915 *Brighton* departing from the station on 6 April 1953, Ramsgate steam shed was opened in stages between 1928 and 1930, and received the BR code 74B under Ashford until 1958, after which it was redesignated 73G under Stewarts Lane until closure the following year. It now serves as a depot for EMUs.

On 13 March 1991 the NSE General Manager's Saloon is seen at the same location, departing for London Victoria and propelled by Class 73/1 No 73109 *Battle of Britain 50th Anniversary*. *R. C. Riley/BM*

BROADSTAIRS: Serving the home of the famed railway traveller Charles Dickens, the station at Broadstairs dates from the opening of the line to Ramsgate in 1863, when the town had a population of less than 2,000. How much the coming of the railway contributed to its present population total of some 22,000 is not known. The line was incorporated by the Herne Bay & Faversham Railway in 1857; the company changed its name to the Margate & London Railway in 1859, and again in 1861, when it became the Kent Coast Railway. From 1871 the route became part of the LC&DR. Heading away from the station with the 15.22 train from Ramsgate, BR Standard Class '5MT' 4-6-0 No 73088 *Joyous Gard* heads for Victoria on 12 March 1959.

Today the area where the sidings have been taken up is completely overgrown, but the lineside trees seem remarkably unchanged as the 09.06 Charing Cross to Margate service (via Ashford and Canterbury West) passes on 18 December 1993, formed of Class '411/5' 4CEP No 1561. *Terry Gough/BM*

MARGATE: The SER opened its 34-mile branch from Ashford to the terminus of Margate Sands in 1846, trains having to reverse at Ramsgate Town. A second station for the town was opened in 1863 on the SE&CR route from Herne Bay to Ramsgate Harbour, and this became Margate & Cliftonville in 1880, Margate West in 1899, and the present-day Margate in 1926, when Margate Sands closed. On 28 June 1953 'Schools' Class 4-4-0 No 30933 *King's Canterbury* pulls away from Margate station with the empty stock of an earlier arrival from Charing Cross.

On 4 July 1992 Class '33/0s' Nos 33026 leading 33040 pass through the station with a ballast train from Tonbridge to Hoo Junction via Canterbury West. One track serving the island platform has been taken out, the embankment has returned to nature, and something akin to what has been described by Royalty as a monstrous carbuncle has appeared on the skyline. *W. A. Corkill/BB*

HERNE BAY: Opened by the Kent Coast Railway in 1861 as Herne Bay & Hampton-on-Sea, the station here is now part of the ex-LC&DR Thanet main line; the Hampton-on-Sea part of the name was dropped in 1951. Departing from the station on an unrecorded date in the early 1950s, BR Standard 'Britannia' Class 'Pacific' No 70004 *William Shakespeare* heads a Ramsgate-Victoria train.

From the same position on 9 May 1993, the Class '423/1' 4VEPs, with No 3446 leading and forming the 13.57 Ramsgate-Victoria train, do not seem to evoke the same majesty, although they are undoubtedly more efficient. The semaphore signal has yielded to a 'colour light', the water tower has of course gone, and the sidings are becoming overgrown from lack of use. *Dr P. Ransome-Wallis/BM*

WHITSTABLE: The changing name of the original Herne Bay & Faversham Railway prior to its purchase by the LC&DR in 1871 resulted in stations only a few miles apart being opened by seemingly different companies, but in fact they were all one and the same. It was the Margate & London Railway that opened the original Whitstable Town station in 1860, although the company became the Kent Coast Railway in the following year. The station name too was changed from 1879 to 1899 when it became Whitstable-on-Sea. A new Whitstable Town station was constructed in 1915, and this became Whitstable & Tankerton in 1936, the Tankerton addition being dropped again in 1979. On 3 August 1958 the 18.12 Ramsgate-Victoria train approaches Whitstable Town station hauled by work-stained rebuilt 'West Country' 'light Pacific' No 34005 *Barnstaple*.

With one arch of the bridge now obscured by a 35-year growth of foliage, and both semaphore signal and telegraph poles having been removed, the 15.57 Ramsgate-Victoria service passes the same location on 9 May 1993, formed by Class '411/5' 4CEPs Nos 1535/1596. *Terry Gough/BM*

WHITSTABLE HARBOUR: The Canterbury & Whitstable Railway was the first public steam-powered passenger and freight line in southern England, and opened in 1830. A little over 6 miles in length, the railway was really of local import, although its freight traffic did survive long enough to become part of the nationalised British Railways. Passenger services ceased under the Southern Railway in January 1931, and complete closure was announced in December 1952. However, the severe floods affecting the Kent Coast line early in 1953 brought about a temporary reopening, and the final train ran in February 1953. With cut-down cab and boiler mountings necessary to pass through Tyler Hill tunnel, Stirling SER-designed 'R1' Class 0-6-0T No 31010 backs two brake-vans into Whitstable Harbour on the last day of scheduled working on the branch, 29 November 1952. Road transport today takes the place of the railway. *Dr P. Ransome-Wallis/BM*

TYLER HILL TUNNEL: Although the Canterbury & Whitstable Railway was only just over 6 miles long, the short route to the coast was required to negotiate the 300-foot plateau of Blean Forest, entailing severe gradients of up to 1 in 31. Beneath Tyler Hill, a 1,012-yard tunnel was bored with extremely limited clearances, requiring any locomotive that used the route to have its standard height reduced in order to pass through safely. Graphically illustrating the situation, the same engine as seen on the opposite page emerges from the southern portal of the tunnel and heads for Canterbury with freight from Whitstable Harbour. The tunnel still exists today, but has been bricked up. *Dr P. Ransome-Wallis/BB*

Medway Valley line

AYLESFORD: The SER's first branch line was from Maidstone Road (now Paddock Wood), following the banks of the River Medway to Maidstone itself (Maidstone West from 1899), and opened in September 1844. The line was extended along the Medway Valley to meet with the SER's North Kent route at Strood in June 1856. The station building at Aylesford dates from the 1856 opening, and is built primarily of Kentish ragstone with leaded windows attributed to a bequest from nearby Aylesford Priory. When seen on 17 May 1986, however, the 130-year-old structure was not in a very good state of repair, as Class '415/1' 4EPB No 5177 arrives forming the 17.44 train from Maidstone West to Strood.

Following a £1/+million restoration in 1988, the building was returned to a representation of its original condition, including replacement of the chimneys. After completion of the work, Class '47/0' No 47197 hauls an engineer's train of life-expired sleepers through the staggered platforms, travelling between Tonbridge and Hoo Junction. *Both BM*

MAIDSTONE WEST: Watering up in the bay platform on 20 August 1959, the fireman of 'H' Class 0-4-4T No 31517 prepares his charge prior to hauling the two 'birdcage' coaches that make up the 18.39 train for Tonbridge.

On 17 July 1993 Class '411/5' 4CEP No 1571 stands in the main platform, with the bay now out of use and completely overgrown. *Terry Gough/BB*

WATERINGBURY: Built by the side of the River Medway, and opened with the first section of the Medway Valley Line, the first train of 25 September 1844 is recorded as stopping at Wateringbury to allow the Band of Lancers to board for Maidstone. Hauling sheeted hoppers through the staggered platforms on 6 April 1960, Bulleid 'Q1' Class 'Austerity' 0-6-0 No 33028 travels tender-first, heading the load from Tonbridge to Maidstone West.

The large brick-built goods shed still stands together with a number of background houses, but the platform building and canopy have been replaced by a steel and glass waiting room, and the platform now appears to be well lit. With the Southern-style station nameboard replaced with one of the NSE variety, similarly attired NSE-liveried Class '411/5' 4CEP No 1563 approaches as the 09.00 train from Tonbridge to Strood on 1 July 1993. *Terry Gough/BM*

PADDOCK WOOD: A station at this location was opened in 1842 as part of the SER's original Dover main line via Redhill and Ashford. With the opening of the branch to Maidstone two years later, the station took the name of a local wood in place of its original title of Maidstone Road, and from 1892 Paddock Wood became a three-way junction when the branch to Hawkhurst opened. On 15 April 1961 'H' Class 0-4-4T No 31324 is in the bay platform on the left with the 12.30 train for Hawkhurst, and on the right No 31500 of the same Class heads the 12.16 Medway Valley line train for Maidstone West.

From the same position on 23 February 1993, the platform canopy is seen to have been truncated, the bay platform area is now the station car park, and the station buildings to the right have been demolished. Only the footbridge remains as the 13.00 Charing Cross-Margate train arrives, formed of Class '411/5' 4CEP No 1598 leading Class '423/1' 4VEP No 3177. *J. C. Haydon/BM*

Hawkhurst branch

HORSMONDEN: Known as the 'Hop Pickers Line', the Cranbrook & Paddock Wood Railway's 11½-mile branch from Paddock Wood through to Hawkhurst was completed in September 1893. It was worked by the SE&CR and absorbed by that company in 1900. A guardless push-pull 12.30 train from Paddock Wood to Hawkhurst arrives at the first station on the line, Horsmonden, on 10 September 1960, with traction provided by 'H' Class 0-4-4T No 31500.

In Closed with the line in 1961, the station area at Horsmonden is now occupied by the Old Station Garage. Part of the original platform now runs through the garage workshop (a station sign is preserved on the wall), the trackbed has returned to nature, and in the same position as the little train is a dumped and wheel-less old Hillman estate car. The oast houses in the background can just be seen through the foliage. *J. H. Aston/BM*

GOUDHURST: The first section of the branch to Hawkhurst was completed through Horsmonden as far as Hope Mill in October 1892. The full name given to the station was 'Hope Mill for Goudhurst and Lamberhurst', but this mouthful was changed in 1892 when the station was renamed as plain Goudhurst. On the last day of operation of the branch, 10 June 1961, Class 'C' 0-6-0 No 31588 departs from Goudhurst heading for Hawkhurst, and passes over the level crossing on the B2079 road.

Apart from an ivy-covered level crossing gatepost, no one would now be aware that a railway had ever existed here. *Stanley Creer/BB*

CRANBROOK: Unlike the station building at Goudhurst, the one at Cranbrook has not been demolished, the 1893 structure having been extended to join with the signal box, and converted to a comfortable home. Before the trackbed became a lawn, the same locomotive and augmented last-day train as shown on the previous page enters Cranbrook station. *R. C. Riley/BM*

HAWKHURST: A number of proposals were made to extend the Hawkhurst branch from its terminus, but all to no avail. The line's dead-end nature robbed it of much utility, the tank engines panting up heavy gradients and through endless hop fields until the four inconveniently sited stations on the line were all closed to traffic on 12 June 1961. It is reported that a million pot plants each year were sent by rail from Hawkhurst, but unfortunately this would not have been sufficient to keep the line open for goods traffic only. On 8 May 1961 Class 'H' 0-4-4T No 31500 is again the rostered engine for the branch, and stands at the terminus waiting to propel its two coaches back to Paddock Wood.

The timber company woodyard once adjacent to Hawkhurst station has now extended to take over the station site, where the goods shed in the background can still be seen as a reference point. Just out of sight behind the timber, Hawkhurst signal box has been nicely preserved. *Chris Gammell/BM*

Uckfield line

EDENBRIDGE TOWN: Once a through route between Victoria and Brighton via Oxted and Lewes, the line was truncated at Uckfield in 1969, and when the connection from Eridge to Tunbridge Wells was also removed, a long branch was created from Hurst Green through to Uckfield, a distance of 25 miles. Edenbridge Town station was one of the original LB&SCR stations on the line and opened in January 1888. On 2 April 1956 Three Bridges-allocated Drummond 'M7' Class 0-4-4T No 30028 departs from the station heading the Oxted to Tunbridge Wells West auto-train.

Yet to be electrified, services on the route are currently operated by DEMUs. On 23 May 1993 the Sunday 08.47 East Croydon-Uckfield train is formed of two Class '205' units, Nos 205018/009. The old goods shed and coal sidings are now fenced off from the railway and occupied by a builders' supplier. Although their residents' view of the railway is slowly disappearing, the houses overlooking the line still remain, albeit with chimney pots reduced in height. *R. C. Riley/BM*

ASHURST: Incorporated by the Brighton, Uckfield & Tunbridge Wells company in 1861, the line north of Uckfield was eventually opened by the LB&SCR in 1888, and included the pleasant station of Ashurst, where Tonbridge-allocated 'H' Class 0-4-4T No 31177 pauses for the scheduled stop with an auto-train from Oxted to Tunbridge Wells West.

With the 12.04 train from Oxted to Uckfield in the station on 23 May 1993, formed of Class '205s' Nos 205009/018, all that appears to remain from the earlier view is the footbridge and the wooden fencing. *M. J. Esau/BM*

BIRCHDEN JUNCTION was once at the lower corner of a triangle of junctions that joined Eridge, Ashurst and Groombridge. When trains for Uckfield all travelled via Tunbridge Wells West, the stretch of line between Ashurst and Birchden Junctions lay unused for many years. However, the closure of the line containing both Groombridge and Tunbridge Wells West resulted in the line from the right being taken out of use, and all Uckfield trains now travel on the track remaining from Ashurst. On 27 December 1986 Class '45/1' 'Peak' No 45104 *The Royal Warwickshire Fusiliers* hauls a railtour for Uckfield through the junction.

At the same position on 1 July 1993 Class '205' DEMU No 205023 forms the 11.05 Oxted-Uckfield service. The lines from the right are severed and out of use, the signal box has gone, and the junction is a junction no more. *Both BB*

UCKFIELD (1): Crossing the Weald through pleasant Sussex countryside, the line from the South Coast to Uckfield was opened by the LB&SCR in 1858, and became a through route between London and Brighton ten years later. Today the station is again a terminus, but this time from the opposite direction, the route south having been truncated in 1969. With a conversation taking place across the level crossing, the 13.12 train for London Victoria departs from Uckfield on 6 May 1980, formed of Class '207' 'East Sussex' DEMU No 1311.

With the station now moved to the other side of the level crossing, and the gates fixed for road priority, a new Uckfield platform has been built (it can hardly be called a station) and the signal box entrance now faces north instead of the original south. In the platform is Class '205' 'Hampshire' DEMU No 205025, having arrived as the 14.04 train from Oxted. *Both BM*

UCKFIELD (2): Having arrived at Uckfield and run round its train, the railtour locomotive depicted on page 108, Class '45/1' 'Peak' No 45104 *The Royal Warwickshire Fusiliers*, prepares for the return journey on the same day.

With the station facilities now moved to the other side of the level crossing, the scene on 18 July 1992 shows what happens to track when neither service nor 'weed-killer' trains operate. The station signs have been taken down, and the lower doors and windows are boarded up. Even the footbridge from which these views were obtained has since been dismantled. *BB/BM*

East Sussex Coast lines

HOVE: Opened by the London & Brighton Railway in 1840 as part of its line to Shoreham, the first Hove station site was situated some half a mile nearer to Brighton than the present structure. It ceased operation as a passenger station in 1880, and became a goods terminal using the name Holland Road. The present station was opened by the LB&SCR (formed in 1846 by the merger of the London & Brighton and the London & Croydon railways) in 1895, and was initially known as Cliftonville. On 5 July 1954 the workmen's train from Lancing Carriage Works, known locally as the 'Lancing Belle', leaves Hove hauled by Wainwright 'D' Class 4-4-0 No 31737 leading bunker-first 'E4' Class 0-6-2T No 32566.

With sidings on both sides of the lines now removed together with signal box and fencing, the 12.46 Littlehampton-Brighton train passes the same place on 27 November 1993, formed by Class '423/1' 4VEP No 3535. *J. H. W. Kent/BM*

PATCHAM: On the main 1841 London-Brighton route just north of Brighton, the picturesque location at Patcham, between Patcham and Clayton tunnels, was a favourite of railway photographers for many years, and the choice for a Victoria-Brighton-Victoria special Pullman run on 28 April 1982. With a pair of Class '73/1' electro-diesels providing power, Nos 73101 *Brighton Evening Argus* and 73142 *Broadlands*, the train is hauled northwards through the lush East Sussex countryside.

At the same location on 27 November 1993 dominance of new road building over rail investment is evident, and the location as a good one for photography has gone. InterCity long-range Class '47/4' No 47807 passes with the 14.20 InterCity train from Brighton to Manchester Piccadilly. A newly erected signal gantry across the lines precludes exactly the same photographic angle being utilised. *BM/BB*

BRIGHTON (1): Although the London to Brighton route opening took place in September 1841, trains had already reached the town from the Shoreham direction since May of the previous year. Brighton station was designed by David Mocatta and is one of the largest on the 'Southern'. It remains essentially unaltered from its early days, although the concourse and platforms have been successively enlarged and lengthened over the years. Departing from the station on 13 April 1958, 'King Arthur' Class 4-6-0 No 30796 *Sir Dodinas le Savage* hauls a Railway Correspondence & Travel Society 58-minute non-stop special to Victoria, while in the station is a 6PUL EMU also for Victoria, painted in standard green livery with a chocolate and cream Pullman car forming the third vehicle.

Much-lengthened platforms and the razing of the Brighton Works buildings adjacent to the station result in an entirely different scene today. *R. C. Riley/BM*

BRIGHTON (2): The difference in the view from Brighton station platforms looking in the opposite direction is even more marked. In April 1959 Class 'A1X' 'Terrier' 0-6-0T No 32635, in LB&SCR livery and carrying the legend 'Brighton Works', shunts a train consisting mainly of BMW Isetta 'bubble cars', which at this time were being made in the Railway Works at Brighton, and moved out from there by rail. The train is alongside the Works buildings, and the footbridge to the signal box and the box itself are both apparent. Currently nothing remains of any structure in this view apart from the trackwork itself. *John C. Baker/BM*

BRIGHTON SHED (75A): Occupying a cramped site to the north-east of the station, the first main Brighton shed constructed in 1841 was closed in 1861, and the buildings incorporated into an expanded Brighton Works. Its replacement was a 16-road shed to the north-west of the station, built on the site of a large chalk cliff which had taken many years to remove. The original tiled and gabled shed roofs were replaced in 1938 by an asbestos covering, but otherwise the site remained relatively unaltered until closure in 1964, when the last few allocated engines were sent to Bournemouth and Guildford. Of the 25 or so locomotives which can be seen on shed on 1 July 1951, at least nine different classes are evident.

Today the area is still occupied by BR, and is in use as an engineering depot for both traffic and civil engineering departments. The building to the rear with the white roof is Lover's Walk EMU Depot. *R. C. Riley/BM*

BRIGHTON WORKS: Dating back to the earliest days of the London & Brighton Railway, the works area at Brighton occupied a 9-acre site adjacent to the station, and from 1852 was heavily involved in locomotive construction, the first, LB&SCR 2-2-2 No 14, emerging in 1852. In all, 1,211 steam engines were built here, the last being BR Standard 2-6-4T No 80154 in March 1957. The Works closed completely in 1964, and in 1971 the site became a very large car park, able to accommodate 1,000 vehicles. Just three of them stand where once Brighton-built 'H2' Class 'Atlantic' No 32421 *South Foreland* was receiving a heavy overhaul on 2 October 1954. *Both BM*

KEMP TOWN: Brighton's only suburban branch was the 1.4-mile line to Kemp Town opened in August 1869, its brief length involving a 14-arch viaduct, a tunnel of over 1,000 yards, and one intermediate station called Lewes Road. Road competition from both trams and buses led to withdrawal of passenger trains from the circuitous route in 1933, but Kemp Town remained open for goods traffic until 1971, Lewes Road station having become a pickle factory. On 23 June 1956 the Stephenson Locomotive Society ran a special excursion to the branch terminus, where Brighton Works' own 'Terrier' 0-6-0T, carrying its Departmental No 377S, provided the motive power. The houses above the cliff and the tunnel mouth remain today as reference points. *R. C. Riley/BB*

FALMER: Situated midway between Brighton and Lewes on the line constructed by the Brighton, Lewes & Hastings Railway (bought out by the LB&SCR prior to opening), the first Falmer station of 1846 was situated on the Lewes side of Falmer tunnel, but was moved to the Brighton side in 1865. Approaching the station on 8 June 1962, rebuilt 'West Country' 'light Pacific' No 34008 *Padstow* heads the 16.40 train from London Bridge to Brighton.

With lineside foliage precluding the same elevation, Class '421/4' 4CIG EMU No 1867 passes the same spot on 27 November 1993, forming the 12.39 service from Eastbourne to Brighton. Today the station is a busy one as it serves nearby Sussex University. *Terry Gough/BM*

LEWES (1): At first called Friar's Walk, the first Lewes station dated from the opening of the double-tracked Brighton, Lewes & Hastings Railway from Brighton in 1846. A new station was built by the LB&SCR in 1857, and this was replaced by the present structure in 1889, which provided for easier curves and better links between the number of routes that now converged here; in addition to the main line in either direction from Brighton and Eastbourne/Hastings, trains arrived from the Tunbridge Wells direction via Uckfield, from Haywards Heath via Keymer Junction, from Seaford, and from the Bluebell Line. Awaiting departure time from Lewes on 7 August 1950, Billinton Class 'E5' 0-6-2T No 2573 (later BR No 32573) has charge of the 11.19 train from Brighton to Tunbridge Wells West.

With the station from this standpoint showing few signs of the 43 intervening years, the 11.15 Brighton-Seaford train awaits departure on 27 November 1993, formed of Class '421/4' 4CIG No 1856. *R. C. Riley/BM*

LEWES (2): Arriving at Lewes on 17 September 1971, 4COR 'Nelson' EMU No 3123 forms a train from Ore to Brighton.

The semaphore signals have now been replaced by 'colour lights', a footbridge has been built behind the signal box, and a house has appeared behind the trees. Everything else, however, appears remarkably unchanged as Class '421/3' 4CIG No 1732 arrives as the 11.04 service from Seaford to Brighton on 27 November 1993. *Both BB*

BERWICK: Situated east of Lewes and opened by the LB&SCR in 1846 as part of the single-track Brighton, Lewes & Hastings Railway's route from Brighton to St Leonards (Bulverhythe), the main claim to fame of Berwick station is that in the 1920s it despatched more milk churns than any other railway station in the south! Departing with the 15.30 Eastbourne-Lewes train on 5 June 1955, it is likely that the crew of BR Standard Class '4MT' 2-6-4T No 80015 would not have been very popular with their Tunbridge Wells West shed colleagues, as this scene was recorded during the national rail strike of that year.

At the same position on 18 September 1993, the 13.55 Eastbourne-Manchester Piccadilly 'InterCity Holidaymaker' service passes through the station at speed, powered by Class '47/4' No 47811. Only the signal remains on the south side of the station, and although the siding is still apparent on the north side, the old plate-layer's hut is a thing of the past. *S. C. Nash/BM*

POLEGATE: Once an important junction between the coast route and the line from London via Eridge and Heathfield, the first station at Polegate dated from 1846, situated on the single line between Lewes and St Leonards (Bulverhythe). After the line was extended to Hastings, and branches were constructed to Eastbourne and Hailsham, however, the station was displaced in 1881 by a new structure some 300 yards to the east. This survived until recent times, when the station was moved again to a site near to the town centre - which is exactly where the original station was situated. On 13 May 1956 'M7' Class 0-4-4T No 30053 passes the second station with a theatrical vans special from Brighton to Hastings, while one of the only six steel-bodied 2HAL EMUs forms the 10.46 train from Brighton to Eastbourne.

With the new station now out of sight around the curve, the 10.51 Victoria-Hastings service passes the same location on 18 September 1993, formed of Class '422/3' 4BIG EMU No 2252. *S. C. Nash/BM*

EASTBOURNE (1): When the single-line branch from Polegate brought the first train to Eastbourne in May 1849, the location was little more than a farming and fishing village. Development soon followed, and the village grew into a town with high residential and holiday resort appeal. Recognising the growth, the LB&SCR resited the original rather spartan station in 1866, and the branch was electrified by the Southern Railway in 1935, when the station was provided with a spacious concourse and the present-day four long platforms. On 2 September 1964 BR Standard Class '4MT' 2-6-4T No 80138 departs from the station with the 08.16 train to Hailsham.

The 'Cuckoo Line' route between Hailsham and Eridge closed to passenger traffic in June 1965, leaving Hailsham as a branch terminus once again, the remaining route between Polegate and Hailsham eventually succumbing in September 1968. With Eastbourne now served only by trains travelling from east and west along the coast, the summer Saturdays only 08.55 'InterCity Holidaymaker Express' to Edinburgh departs on 18 September 1993, hauled by Class '47/4' No 47828, which will take the train as far as Birmingham New Street, where an electric locomotive will take over. The 'sensor' protruding from the locomotive is a lamp standard for the carriage sidings, unfortunately placed to photograph a train in exactly the same position as in the earlier scene! *G. D. King/BB*

EASTBOURNE (2): Approaching Eastbourne on 8 August 1961, Billinton 'K' Class 'Mogul' No 32340 hauls five 'Southern' coaches forming a summer train from Wolverhampton Low Level to Hastings. Requiring to reverse at Eastbourne terminus, another engine of the same class, No 32342, waits in the background to take the train forward to its destination.

At the same position on 18 September 1993, the 07.51 Victoria-Hastings train is formed of Class '421/4' 4CIG stock, No 1835 leading No 1831. Without the need to shunt-release the engine or to attach another one at the other end of the train prior to reversal, the present-day movements for electric stock are accomplished with much greater efficiency, but without the spectacle. Currently only two tracks remain here, with a third allowing coaching stock to travel through the washing plant. With the brickwork now faced, a number of the background houses remain, but the old coal sidings and depot are now a car park. *P. J. Lynch/BM*

EASTBOURNE SHED (75G): A modest two-road shed was constructed close to Eastbourne station in 1849 to coincide with the opening of the line. This was replaced on the same site by an eight-stall roundhouse in 1876. This lasted until 1912, when the LB&SCR built a seven-road shed some distance from the station, which retained a locomotive allocation of its own until 1952, when the engines were distributed between Brighton, Tunbridge Wells West, Redhill and St Leonards. The building was then classified as a Brighton sub-shed but a serious fire in 1956 resulted in it becoming virtually roofless, after which it further deteriorated, with final closure occurring in 1965. Where the line of stored BR Standard Class '4MT' 2-6-4Ts were stored outside the derelict shed in 1965, all that remains today are a few bricks strewn among the wasteland. *Stanley Creer/BM*

BEXHILL: Another station situated on the original single line between Lewes and St Leonards (Bulverhythe), Bexhill first opened on the present site in June 1846, and served the small village of that name which was clustered around an ancient parish church over a mile from the coast; the present Bexhill-on-Sea resort came about much later. Given the title of Bexhill Central to avoid confusion with the SER station which opened on the west side of the town in 1902, the present building dates from 1901. Leaving the station on the evening of 14 July 1960, a return Sunday school special for Hailsham is hauled by Brighton (75A)-based 'E4' Class 0-6-2T No 32515.

Passing the same Playhouse Cinema building on 15 November 1993, Class '421/4' 4CIG No 1860 forms the 12.28 Hastings-Victoria service. It is no longer possible to obtain the same photographic angle from lineside, as the siding has now been developed, and the high brick wall on the extreme left is part of a large supermarket complex. *S. C. Nash/BM*

BEXHILL WEST: Inaugurated by the Crowhurst, Sidley & Bexhill Railway in 1897, the 4½-mile branch line linking Crowhurst, Sidley and Bexhill to the SER main line was opened by the SER in June 1902. Opened as 'Bexhill', the station name was changed to Bexhill-on-Sea in 1920, reverted to plain Bexhill in 1923, and finally became Bexhill West in 1929. Through services from Charing Cross ran on the branch until 1940, but thereafter a shuttle operated from Crowhurst, operated by DEMUs from 1958 until the line closed in 1964. Operating the shuttle on 15 July 1950, Stroudley 'D3' Class 0-4-4T No 32388 awaits the scheduled departure time before setting out for Crowhurst.

The terminus building still stands today, and is now used by 'Fryer's Auction Galleries'. *R. C. Riley/BM*

NEWHAVEN: A 6-mile branch line from Southerham Junction, just over a mile east of Lewes, was opened to what is now Newhaven Town station by the LB&SCR in 1847, and extended another 2½ miles to Seaford in 1864 (see page 2). The railway company confidently expected Newhaven to become a great port, in fact the 'Liverpool of the South' according to an 1852 guide book, and under the auspices of the LB&SCR the Newhaven Harbour Company was created in 1878, and Newhaven Harbour station opened in 1886 in place of Newhaven Wharf. Following many improvements to harbour facilities, sailings began in 1889, the steamers having become railway property in 1867. The Harbour Company was vested in the Southern Railway in 1926, became a part of BR upon nationalisation, and is now operated by Stena Sealink Line, who have two sailings a day to Dieppe, both currently connected by boat trains from London Victoria. Heading away from Newhaven with the 16.52 boat train from Harbour station to Victoria on 27 August 1951 is Earle-Marsh 'H2' Class 'Atlantic' No 32426 *St Alban's Head*.

At the same location on 18 September 1993 the 18.30 Seaford-Brighton train is formed of Class '421/3' 4CIG No 1723. With the signal box from which the earlier photograph was taken being no longer there, the same elevation was not available. *R. C. Riley/BM*

NEWHAVEN SWING BRIDGE: A freight tramway on the right bank of the River Ouse was built to West Quay as part of the improvements to Newhaven Harbour. Weight restrictions on the swing bridge over the river were such as to make the line the sole prerogative of the little 'A1X' Class 'Terrier' 0-6-0Ts, one of which, No 32670, makes the crossing on 25 October 1958.

The line across the river closed in 1963, and while the now rusted gates are still evident, the swing bridge beyond has been demolished. *W. M. J. Jackson/BB*

NEWHAVEN SHED: The original LB&SCR two-road engine shed at Newhaven was superseded by a larger four-road structure adjacent to Newhaven Town station in 1887. It provided motive power for main-line trains to London, and local services to Seaford, Lewes and Brighton. It became a sub-shed under Brighton prior to allocation of BR shed codes, and consequently never received one of its own. Simmering outside the shed on a sunny 2 October 1954 are 'Terrier' 0-6-0T No 32636 and 'E4' Class 0-6-2T No 32513.

Closure of the shed came about in 1960, and the site is now occupied as the Newhaven Port engineer's yard. The distinctive shed roofs are still apparent. *Both BM*

Cuckoo Line

MAYFIELD: The branches north and south from Polegate, to Hailsham and Eastbourne respectively, were both opened by the LB&SCR on 14 May 1849, a service between the two villages being provided via Polegate in either direction. Hailsham remained a terminus for 31 years until the line was extended to join with Eridge in 1880, providing access to Tunbridge Wells. Opened with the extension in 1880, the Mayfield platforms were looking rather uncared for on 16 August 1962 as the almost inevitable BR Standard Class '4MT' 2-6-4T, this time No 80037, paused for custom with the 12.45 train from Eastbourne to Tunbridge Wells West.

Closure of the extension from Hailsham to Eridge together with the stations of Hellingly, Horam, Heathfield, Mayfield, and Rotherfield & Marks Cross took place in June 1965. The station building on the left remains as a private residence, but the platforms and trackbed have been totally removed and the area is now an overgrown embankment to the road below. *Terry Gough/BM*

HEATHFIELD: The Cuckoo Line was so named because of the Cuckoo Fair held annually on 14 April at Heathfield to herald the approaching summer. Entering the station with an Eastbourne-bound train on 28 September 1963, BR Standard '4MT' 2-6-4T No 80094, passes another local service for Tunbridge Wells West formed of an 'East Sussex' DEMU.

All trace of the station has disappeared since the 1965 closure, and residents requiring public transport are now obliged to use the roads. On 25 September 1993 a well-loaded bus passes the same location; the houses above it still remain to provide a reference. *John Faulkner/BM*

132

ROTHERFIELD & MARKS CROSS (1): Closed together with the other 'Cuckoo Line' stations north of Hailsham from June 1965, the station building at Rotherfield & Marks Cross is now a well-appointed private residence. Many disused stations have been put to use in this way, but this example is quite exceptional in that the owner is sympathetic to the ideals of preservation in general, even the station canopy being retained as a verandah. On 4 September 1953 the 10.42 train from Tunbridge Wells West to Eastbourne enters the station hauled by Ivatt Class '2MT' 'Mickey Mouse' 2-6-2T No 41318. One solitary passenger waits to board. *R. C. Riley/BM*

ROTHERFIELD & MARKS CROSS (2): With a camera pointed in the opposite direction from the view on the previous page, another 'Mickey Mouse' tank, No 41316, arrives at the station on 3 October 1953, hauling a stopping train from Eastbourne to Tunbridge Wells West.

Not only has the present owner of the station building retained many aspects of the original, but even the platform edges are still evident, flanking a sunken garden which was once the trackbed. *Stanley Creer/BM*

Kent & East Sussex Railway

HEADCORN: Although the SER projected its lines from Tonbridge to Ashford, and via Tunbridge Wells and Robertsbridge to Hastings, the company was seemingly uninterested in seeking a connection to the important and ancient town of Tenterden. Even the Light Railway Act of 1896 did not prompt the company to extend its system in this direction, and it was an independent Rother Valley (Light) Railway under the direction of Holman F. Stephens (later Lieutenant-Colonel), who became the railway's Managing Director, which constructed the first section of the line from Robertsbridge to what is now known as Rolvenden. The railway ran its first trains in April 1900, the first operational light railway worked by an independent company. The extension to Tenterden Town was completed in 1902, and in 1904 the section to Headcorn opened to traffic under the company's new title of the Kent & East Sussex Railway (K&ESR).

Awaiting custom from a connecting London train at Headcorn on 28 November 1953, Stirling 'O1' Class 0-6-0 No 31065 has charge of a typical two-coach train of the period.

At Headcorn today, the bay platform and sidings have been reclaimed by nature. *Stanley Creer/BM*

HIGH HALDEN ROAD station opened in 1905 with the section of line between Tenterden Town and Headcorn. The K&ESR passed into the hands of BR at nationalisation in 1948 and closure followed, with the line between Headcorn and Robertsbridge running its last service trains in January 1954, and the route from Tenterden to Robertsbridge following in June 1961. The stations of Tenterden St Michaels, High Halden Road, Biddenden and Frittenden Road, together with the connection to Headcorn, remain a memory, but of course the line south from Tenterden has been re-opened in stages from 1974 by the Tenterden Railway Company, now known as the Kent & East Sussex Steam Railway.

Hauling just one ex-London & South Western Railway coach, the same Class 'O1' 0-6-0 as seen on the previous page makes the High Halden Road stop on 4 August 1952, with the 08.50 train from Headcorn to Robertsbridge.

The station building and platform still stand today in private hands, but sadly there is no longer a rail connection, and the K&ESR hand-operated signal has gone. *P. J. Lynch/BM*

TENTERDEN TOWN (1): Lt-Col Stephens's untimely death in 1931 brought to an end any question of the railway extending its operations, and by 1936 the condition of its own locomotives made it necessary to hire motive power from the Southern Railway. On 27 July 1953 Class 'A1X' 'Terrier' 0-6-0T No 32655 arrives at Tenterden Town station with a service from Robertsbridge to Headcorn.

Apart from the second platform having being removed, the picture of 'Terrier' No 32650 taken over 40 years later has hardly changed at all, a tribute to the preservationists who have worked so hard to restore and maintain the line. *R. C. Riley/BM*

TENTERDEN TOWN (2): The climb from Rolvenden to Tenterden Town is constructed on a rising gradient of 1 in 50, a severe test for any motive power working the line, particularly when the rails are greasy. Approaching the station over the old level crossing on 27 July 1953, tender-first 'O1' Class 0-6-0 No 31370 hauls a Robertsbridge-Headcorn train past the hand-operated signals and the 'Whistle' board.

At the same position on New Year's Day 1993, Hunslet 0-6-0ST No 24 *William H. Austen* tops the climb with the 13.45 train from Northiam. The whole area has been nicely tidied up, and proper crossing gates installed. *R. C. Riley/BM*

ROBERTSBRIDGE: The Kent & East Sussex Steam Railway is still in the process of extending its line south to reach Robertsbridge again, and currently has services running as far as Northiam. It is hoped that this scene at Robertsbridge on 22 July 1953 will be able to be recaptured again in the not too distant future, and that once again there will be an interchange here with the BR main line. Fronting the 08.15 departure from Robertsbridge on 22 July 1953, 'A1X' Class 'Terrier' No 32655 moves away with its single coach for Tenterden Town.

On a very wet 29 December 1993, the sidings are now the station car park, but the line into the bay platform still exists, as the 09.10 train from Hastings to Charing Cross arrives at the main-line platform formed of Class '423/1' 4VEP No 3545. *R. C. Riley/BM*

Bluebell Railway

SHEFFIELD PARK (1): North of Sheffield Park station, the Bluebell Railway comes within the boundaries of West Sussex, and the line from there through Horsted Keynes to East Grinstead is included in Vol 16 of the 'British Railways Past & Present' series, covering Surrey and West Sussex. The southern half of the line from Sheffield Park to Culver Junction, north of Lewes, was opened on behalf of the Lewes & East Grinstead Railway by the LB&SCR in August 1882. Known initially as the 'Bluebell & Primrose Line', the railway was a very busy one, but started to decline in the 1920s and struggled on to become a part of BR in 1948. The route was closed in May 1955, but had to be reopened again after the closure was found to be illegal, and a second closure took place after Ministry intervention in March 1958. The line from Sheffield Park to Horsted Keynes became the first standard gauge passenger line to be taken over by enthusiasts, and the route is currently being extended to East Grinstead. The track south from near Sheffield Park, however, was lifted in 1959/60, and there are no plans for restoration in this direction.

On 27 March 1954 a football excursion from East Grinstead to Lewes leaves Sheffield Park hauled by Class 'C2X' 'Vulcan' 0-6-0 No 32539.

At the same position now is situated the impressive engine shed and workshops of the Bluebell Railway. *S. C. Nash/BM*

SHEFFIELD PARK (2): Following considerable organisation for funding and purchase from BR, restoration of the line and buildings commenced, and to packed platforms the first trains on the preserved Bluebell Railway ran on 7 August 1960 - and have been running with increasing success ever since. In the distance, running into Sheffield Park station on 27 March 1950, is a Wainwright 'Mogul' with a train for East Grinstead.

Another Wainwright 'Mogul', 'U' Class No 1618, restored in Southern Railway livery, awaits departure on 24 April 1993 for a temporary stopping place just south of Kingscote; services to the beautifully restored Kingscote station recommenced in 1994. Apart from a footbridge being installed in place of the wooden foot crossing, and a viewing enclosure now being provided, the present-day scene could almost have been taken in the 1930s - but then that is what preservation is all about. *R. C. Riley/BM*

BARCOMBE: The stations south of Sheffield Park which finally closed to traffic in 1958 were Newick & Chailey and Barcombe. Barcombe today is a delightfully appointed private residence, slightly obscured from the overlooking road bridge by the branch of a large tree. From the same bridge on 2 September 1953 ex-LB&SCR 'E4' Class 0-6-2T No 32520 leaves the platform with its three-coach East Grinstead-Lewes train. Barcombe station used to be the busiest on the route, but never reopened again after the initial attempt by BR to close the line in 1955.
R. C. Riley/BM

Lavender Line

ISFIELD: The line from the South Coast to Uckfield was opened by the LB&SCR in 1858, and included stations at Barcombe Mills and Isfield. Eventually the route was connected to London by way of Eridge, and either Tunbridge Wells or Oxted, but the southern section was abandoned in 1969, leaving Uckfield as a terminus from the north. Part of the original trackbed to the south is now preserved in the hands of the Lavender Line, and trains operate again between Isfield and a location to the north known as Dingley Dell. Before closure was contemplated, this was how Isfield station looked on 13 March 1950.

On 24 April 1993 the top of the station building can be seen above the preserved Class '115' DMU, and the station platform is now neat and cared for. *R. C. Riley/BM*

INDEX OF LOCATIONS